CARDIFF IN WALES
2005


100 years a City
50 years a Capital


John May

# CARDIFF IN WALES 2005
© John May 2004

ISBN 1 871354 10 2

Published by Castle Publications,
17 Mill Road, Tongwynlais, Cardiff CF15 7JP, UK
Tel: 029 2081 1603   Fax: 029 2081 1049

Printed by
Lazy Cat Productions, Caerphilly CF83 1BQ

# CONTENTS

# PICTURE CREDITS

Cover photographs of the Millennium Stadium, the Millennium Centre, Cardiff Bay Barrage and Lake, and St. David's Hotel and Spa by Nick Jenkins, Freespirit Images, Cardiff.

Photographs on pages 41-44 by courtesy of the National Museums and Galleries of Wales and Cardiff County Council.

John May is the author of three previous publications about Cardiff -

THE CARDIFF QUIZ BOOK
MILLENNIUM CARDIFF
CARDIFF DAY-BY-DAY

and has written numerous other books of Welsh interest -

THE TWENTIETH CENTURY WELSH QUIZ BOOK
THE YEARBOOK OF WELSH DATES
REFERENCE WALES*
A CHRONICLE OF WELSH EVENTS*
QUIZ RHONDDA
THE NEWPORT CITY QUIZ BOOK
A BOOK OF WELSH BIRTHPLACES*
RHONDDA 1203 - 2003

all published by Castle Publications except those starred*

The author is a Cardiff University graduate in history.
After teaching in further education in South Wales for some years he now works in tourism and is based in Cardiff.

# INTRODUCTION

Cardiff is becoming increasingly well known, particularly through its high sporting profile, with major events staged in the soaring Wales Millennium Stadium, and through prestigious developments in the arts led by the vast new Wales Millennium Centre for the Performing Arts in Cardiff Bay. There are also richly rewarded international competitions for singers and for artists which attract world-wide participation and interest.

There can be few places able to enjoy such favourable recognition, an ongoing major waterfront regeneration - one of the most ambitious in Europe - and at the same time celebrate the anniversaries of two important changes in status, first to city and then to capital city, as Cardiff is able to do in 2005.

This souvenir publication looks at the background to these milestones in Cardiff's growth, lists a wide range of facts about the city together with many observations and comments on it. The two major dates of 1905 and 1955 are set against a background of events elsewhere in Wales, in Britain and in the world in general.

Those eager to test their knowledge of Cardiff in the early twentieth century, the mid twentieth century and the early years of the present century can take up the challenge of three quiz sets, each with 70 questions.

All that is needed to be known about Cardiff to savour the celebrations of 2005 will be found in these pages. Enjoy !

John May
Tongwynlais
Cardiff

August 2004

To my colleagues in tourism in the city
flying the flag for Cardiff.

## A COUNTRY WITHOUT A CITY
## Wales Before 1905

Through most of the 2,000 years following the Roman Conquest in the first century AD, when its inhabitants probably numbered between 50,000 and 100,000, Wales had a small, scattered population with few towns of any great size let alone cities. The first town, Caerwent, was founded by the Romans for the South Wales tribe, the Silures, and it probably had a peak population of about 3,000 to 4,000, but this declined after the Romans left in the late fourth century AD to become a very small settlement. Not for 1,300 years until the late seventeenth century did Wales again have another town, Wrexham, with a population as great as that of Roman Caerwent.

Until the eighteenth century and the coming of industry, Wales had no major centres of population and it has been estimated that in 1550 only 12 places had populations of over 1,000 - the largest being Carmarthen with 2,150, Brecon with 1,750 and Wrexham with 1,515. By the late seventeenth century Wrexham had become the largest Welsh town with over 3,000 inhabitants followed by Carmarthen (2,195), Brecon and Haverfordwest (about 2,000 each).

In 1700 in Britain as a whole, only three places outside London had populations of over 20,000 - Bristol, Edinburgh and Norwich - while Birmingham and Glasgow had between 10,000 and 15,000 each. The great majority of the British population lived in small towns with under 5,000 inhabitants or in villages and hamlets and on farms.

### Cardiff Accelerates

Cardiff lagged behind many other towns in Wales in growth until the second half of the nineteenth century and in each of the censuses from the first in 1801 to that of 1861, the returns showed that Merthyr Tydfil was the biggest town in Wales - a long way ahead of any other place in 1801 when it had a population of 7,700. Cardiff, which had only 1,870 inhabitants in 1801, did not overtake Merthyr Tydfil until 1871 when the seaport's population reached 57,363 and it has had the greatest population in Wales ever since.

Although by the late nineteenth century Wales had other large towns like Carmarthen, Newport, Pembroke, Swansea and Wrexham, it still lacked a major centre with the title of city not dependent on being the seat of a bishop and with a lord mayor.

When Cardiff entered the twentieth century its population had soared to 164,000 and it had become one of the most dynamic commercial centres in Britain with the building of a prestigious civic centre underway. Its confidence in its future was boundless and its ambitions unlimited.

It was one of the world's busiest sea ports, it had a University College, a Coal and Shipping Exchange  bustling with traders, six theatres, three daily newspapers, a strikingly rebuilt castle, department stores, enthusiastically supported sports clubs, attractive shopping arcades, smart restaurants, imposing hotels, an infirmary, army barracks, a large covered central market, a handsome new General Post Office in Portland stone, one of the largest multi-racial communities in Britain, an indoor swimming pool, a horse-racing track, a prison, a large central library with a museum, a new electric tram service, a fast rail connection to London through the Severn Tunnel - everything that could be expected to be found in a major urban centre was in Cardiff. Its international importance was shown by the presence of some 30 consulates and vice-consulates.

The town's energetic campaign to be made a city met with success when a charter was granted by King Edward VII on 23 October 1905.

**In just two generations Cardiff had gone from being a small, obscure Welsh coastal town to become a thriving cosmopolitan metropolis on the way to becoming a capital.**

## A COUNTRY WITHOUT A CAPITAL
### Wales Before 1955

Wales had never had a capital in its long history before this title was bestowed on Cardiff in 1955 by Queen Elizabeth II. In the Middle Ages Wales had not been a united country and was controlled by competing rulers in Deheubarth, Gwynedd, Powys and Morganwg, each holding his own court and gradually losing territory to Anglo-Norman invaders. With the final conquest and subjugation of Wales by Edward I following the death in combat in Powys of Prince Llywelyn ap Gruffydd in 1282, the idea of a capital became irrelevant.

Centres of royal administration for the conquered land were set up in Caernarfon for the north and in Carmarthen for the south but some 50 Marcher lordships in Wales were outside this royal control. During the rebellion of Owain Glyndŵr from 1400 to 1415 (the Third Welsh War of Independence), Parliaments were summoned by Owain as Prince of Wales at Machynlleth and Harlech which, together with Aberystwyth, became temporary centres of administration.

Towards the end of the fifteenth century, because of the lawless conditions prevailing and as more Marcher lordships passed into royal hands, a Council for Wales and the Marches was created in 1471 to stablise the restless country. Its administrative centre was the Shropshire border town of Ludlow and the Council continued to function there until it was abolished in 1689.

In the meantime the so-called Acts of Union of 1536 and 1543 had been passed with the intention of absorbing Wales into England and London was clearly the capital of this intended expansion of England.

**National Awareness**
However, the development of Welsh national consciousness from the late eighteenth century, part of the European-wide

Romantic movement, led to the first national institutions being created in Wales. The National Eisteddfod of Wales, in its present form, dates from 1861 and the University of Wales with colleges at Aberystwyth, Bangor and Cardiff, was created in 1893. Then followed the National Library of Wales in Aberystwyth and the National Museum of Wales in Cardiff, both receiving their charters in 1907. The Central Welsh Board (CWB) was established in Cardiff in 1896 as a school inspectorate and examinations body for the whole of Wales.

Cardiff was elevated to city status in 1905, the leading administrative and commercial centre in Wales and the hub of the country's most important industry at the time - coal.
A Welsh Board of Education was established in the new city in 1907, followed by the Welsh National Insurance Commission in 1912 and by the Welsh Board of Health and the Welsh Board of Agriculture, both in 1919.

Cardiff became the seat of a Roman Catholic archdiocese in 1916, the Welsh Council of the League of Nations was established in the city in 1922, the Welsh School of Architecture was founded in Cardiff in 1925, the National Museum was opened in 1927, the Welsh National War Memorial was unveiled in Alexandra Gardens in 1928 and the Welsh National School of Medicine was founded in Cardiff in 1931. The city became the headquarters of the new BBC Welsh Home Service in 1937 and during World War Two Cardiff was the Welsh regional headquarters for civil defence.

After the war Cardiff housed the regional headquarters of the nationalised coal, electricity, gas and rail industries as well as the Wales Hospital Board and in 1946 Welsh National Opera was founded in the city. From 1948 to 1969 the advisory Council for Wales met in Cardiff.

## A New Status

These developments led to a call for the city to be recognised as the capital of Wales although there was some opposition from other claimants to the title like Aberystwyth and Caernarfon. Eventually the pressure was successful and official recognition came on 20 December 1955 - a capital Christmas present for Cardiff which by then had a population of some 250,000.

.

Many Welsh national organisations were subsequently established in Cardiff including the Welsh Arts Council in 1967, the Welsh Sports Council in 1972, the Wales TUC in 1973, the Welsh Consumer Council in 1975, the Welsh Development Agency in 1976, the Institute of Welsh Affairs in 1987 and the Welsh Language Board in 1988. Cardiff was the obvious choice for the location of the National Assembly for Wales when it was established in 1999.

Wales is not alone among European countries in obtaining a capital late in its existence. Switzerland had no capital until Berne was chosen in 1849 and Albania not until 1912 when Tirana acquired this status, while Vitoria did not become the Basque capital until 1979.

# CARDIFF AND THE SEA

Cardiff's historical connection with the sea began with the Roman Conquest of Wales in the first century AD. Roman ships were able to sail up the River Taff, whose course was about 100 yards or metres further to the east than it is now, to supply the fort built on the site today occupied by Cardiff Castle at a suitable point for fording the river at low tide. In the centuries that followed the withdrawal of the Romans at the end of the fourth century AD, Viking raids and perhaps settlement took place along the South Wales coast. The name 'Womanby' in central Cardiff may indicate a Viking habitation - it is Norse for 'huntsmen's dwelling' ('hundemanby'). Flat Holm is another example of a Norse or Viking name, 'holm' meaning island.

The Norman castle built on the site of the Roman fort in the eleventh century after the defeat of the local Welsh was again able to be supplied up the Taff. It is this combination of fortification and river which has given us the place name Cardiff or Caerdydd - 'the fort on the Taff'.

In the Middle Ages a small walled town grew up around the castle and a number of quays were built on the banks of the former course of the Taff where the eastern side of Westgate Street is today, hence Quay Street at right angles to Westgate Street opposite the main entrance area to the Millennium Stadium. The river was dredged regularly to allow ships of up to 80 tons to travel the two miles or three kilometres up the Taff from its mouth to the town when the tide was in. There were also smaller landing places for vessels at Leckwith Bridge on the River Ely and at Rumney Bridge on the River Rumney.

The Glamorganshire Canal, opened in 1794 to link the coast with the South Wales interior, could handle ships of up to 200 tons entering it through the canal's sea lock, in effect a dock. Ships too large for the lock could be loaded out at sea in the Cardiff Roads from lighters.

## Dock Building

Cardiff's reputation as one of the world's major ports began to be acquired only from the 1840s following the opening in 1839 of the first of the five Bute docks, the Bute West (originally called the Bute Ship Canal) built by the Scottish aristocrat, the second Marquis of Bute. By the time that the second dock, the Bute East, was completed in the late 1850s and coal berths constructed on the east bank of the River Ely, the River Taff had been straightened by 'the New Cut' engineered by Isambard Kingdom Brunel. This led to the abandoning of the town's old quays from which agricultural products from the Vale of Glamorgan had been shipped across to Bristol and elsewhere.

By the end of the nineteenth century, when there were four docks in Cardiff, the town had become one of the greatest of the world's seaports and this development continued into the twentieth century with the completion of the largest of the five Cardiff Bute docks, the Alexandra, in 1907. This gave Cardiff a total wet dock area of 162 acres (65 hectares). The port could deal with up to  80 vessels at any one time and in 1913, the peak year for coal exports of some 10.5 million tons, over 7,600 ships were handled. At times the port was so busy that ships might have to wait at anchor in Cardiff Roads for two or three days until there were berths available for them.

The main imports through the port were large quantities of iron ore for the Dowlais steel works on Cardiff's East Moors and Scandinavian timber pit props for the coal mines in the valleys. In the peak year for this Scandinavian trade, 1908, just over one million pit props were imported.

The docks area became the home of thousands of incomers from all parts of the world. It gained a nickname, Tiger Bay, together with a reputation for its vibrant and colourful but sometimes seamy and violent character.

## Ship Building and Ship Repairing

Although some 100 ships were built in Cardiff, the town never became an important shipbuilding centre to rival Barrow, Belfast, Tyneside or the Clyde. But Cardiff did become a major ship repair centre and at one time there were 12 dry docks in the port, now all gone. Repairs were also carried out at the 'dolphins', the distinctive wooden structures near the Norwegian Church where vessels' hulls could be worked on when the tide was out. This was a cheaper option than using a dry dock. In 1910, the peak year for ship repairs in the port, 1,035 vessels had work completed on them.

At the height of maritime activity at the port Cardiff was the world's tramp steamer capital and the Cardiff Shipowners' Association was formed as early as 1875. In 1920 there were 120 shipping companies in the city and almost 400 vessels were registered in the port. However, decline set in from the 1930s with a calamitous fall in world-wide demand for South Wales coal but all five docks remained open. In the late 1920s and early 1930s attempts were made to develop Cardiff as a passenger terminal for trans-Atlantic Cunard and White Star liners but this experiment proved unsuccessful.

Cardiff recognised the importance of shipping to the city by granting its Freedom to two of its leading shipowners, Lord Glanely (William James Tatem) and Sir William Reardon Smith in 1928.

Cardiff had a new lease of life during World War Two handling military supplies and some 15,000 people - women as well as men - were employed although further decline set in rapidly after 1945. Both of the city's oldest docks, the Bute West and the Bute East were closed, in 1964 and 1970 respectively. The Bute West was filled in during 1972 - it was just to the east of the apartments on Lloyd George Avenue - while Bute East was cut off at its southern end near County Hall leaving the port with three working docks.

From 1887 to 1972, except for the war years, the pleasure steamers of P. and A. Campbell took many thousands of people every year on trips along the Bristol Channel coast from Pierhead, a service now run from Penarth Pier. At one time Cardiff was a significant commercial fishing port with a fleet of trawlers and drifters operating out of Bute West Dock from 1888 but the last catch of fish was landed here in 1956.

## Nautical Names

The Cardiff Bay area abounds in reminders of Cardiff's maritime past. There is a large multi-racial community at its core in Butetown or Tiger Bay, attracted to Cardiff by its world-wide links. The Merchant Navy Memorial - shared with Barry and Penarth - stands outside the National Assembly for Wales's new debating chamber while there is a Merchant Navy Mural near Techniquest, the leading scientific exhibition centre. The Norwegian Church shows Cardiff's once strong links with Scandinavia and the names of older Cardiff pubs are resonant with reminders of the maritime world: the Ship and Pilot, the Packet, the Paddle Steamer and the Yardarm. Newer pubs like the Wharf and the Waterguard maintain the naming custom.

Cardiff still remains a general cargo port, its shipping unaffected by the Cardiff Bay barrage. Although its great days have gone, it is the location of the Seafarers' International Research Centre and the home port of RMS *St Helena*, the mail steamer which four times a year sails with passengers to the islands of the South Atlantic. Cardiff has an older association with the southern hemisphere as it was from the port that Captain Robert Scott's ill-fated expedition to the South Pole sailed in June, 1910. Scott's association with Cardiff, whose wealthy businessmen substantially financed the expedition, is remembered in the memorial lighthouse in Roath Park Lake, built in 1918, and in the Antarctic statue near the Norwegian Church unveiled in 2003. A year before Scott's departure, a party led by the geologist Edgeworth (later Sir Edgeworth) David from St Fagans, had become the first to reach the magnetic South Pole.

Royal Navy ships make regular courtesy visits to Cardiff and none has been more popular than the guided missile destroyer HMS *Cardiff*, the third warship to bear this name, and which was given the Freedom of Cardiff in 1988.

Cardiff recognised its indebtedness to the sailors of the merchant service by granting the Freedom of the city to the Merchant Navy in 2001.

After reclaiming land from the sea and the foreshore with the building of the five Bute docks between 1839 and 1907, Cardiff's interface with the ocean was changed even more drastically from November 1999 with the completion of the Cardiff Bay barrage. Three quarters of a mile (1,100 metres) long, it took over five years to build this impressive civil engineering construction which impounded the waters of the River Taff and the River Ely to create a 500 acre (200 hectare) fresh water lake with a circumference of almost eight miles (13 kilometres) and which ended the millennia-long careers of the two rivers as tidal waters.

# CARDIFF AND COAL

One product of the industrial world became intimately connected with Cardiff - the 'black gold' from the South Wales valleys, coal.

Small quantities of coal had been brought down to the coast by pack horses and mules for many years before the Glamorganshire Canal was opened in 1794, the Taff Vale Railway in 1840 and the Rhymney Railway in 1858. But Cardiff's first major export from the valleys was not coal but iron, the reason for the building of the Glamorganshire Canal, 25 miles (40 kilometres) long between the coast and Merthyr Tydfil. This was the centre of the most important iron producing area in Britain in the late eighteenth and early nineteenth century.

Major changes came with the discovery of rich deposits of coal, especially steam coal from the Rhondda valleys, from the 1850s although the tonnage of coal carried on the Glamorganshire Canal exceeded that of iron for the first time as early as 1830. However, it was to be another quarter of a century before the value of coal exports exceeded that of iron.

Cardiff's amazing population growth during the nineteenth century is a vivid indication of the burgeoning coal trade. When the third Marquis of Bute was born in 1847, the population of Cardiff was almost 18,000 and there was only one dock in the town, opened by his father in 1839. By the time of the third Marquis's death in 1900 the population had increased to 164,000 - a nine fold increase - and there were four Bute docks in the port. Over the same years the annual quantity of coal shipped out had increased from just under one million tons to just over eight million tons and Cory Brothers of Cardiff had established 80 bunkering depots for South Wales coal in all parts of the world.

## Peak Years

Cardiff was at the centre of the huge South Wales coal industry which at its peak in the early 1920s employed some 270,000 miners in over 600 mines and which exported a greater proportion of its output than any other British coalfield. The price of coal was fixed in the ornate Coal and Shipping Exchange opened in 1886 in the heart of the docklands. For many years, the price of coal directly determined miners' wages so the standard of living of miners and their wives and children was decided on by a small number of men agreeing contracts in Cardiff docks.

In the mining industry's heyday long coal trains continuously clanked their way through the city to the docks and extensive railway sidings had to be constructed on the outskirts of Cardiff to handle the thousands of coal trucks. The city's three rivers, the Ely, the Rumney and the Taff - now supporting healthy fish populations - became polluted with black coal dust.

At one time there were 65 coal staithes for loading ships and an army of thousands of dock workers like the tippers who operated the dockside machinery and the trimmers who stowed coal aboard ships. Today all the coal staithes have gone, the coal handlers have long departed the waterfront and fewer than 100 people are now employed in the docks. **The very last cargo of coal to leave Cardiff was shipped out from Alexandra Dock in August 1964.**

The great South Wales coalfield, at one time the biggest of the British coalfields producing 20 per cent of the country's coal, is now a mere shadow of its former self. Fewer than 2,000 men are still employed in the mining industry which did so much to make Cardiff the important place it is today. For some 30 years betweeen 1954 and 1983 the annual South Wales Miners' Gala at Sophia Gardens, preceeded by a march from the Civic Centre through the city with lodge banners and brass bands, was a regular reminder to Cardiff of the original basis of the city's wealth. From 1898 to 1970 the headquarters building of the South Wales miners was in Cardiff and the city acknowledged the importance of the miners by honouring the South Wales Area of the National Union of Mineworkers with its Freedom in 1995.

Many years before this Cardiff had conferred its Freedom on two of the local 'coal barons', Lord Merthyr (William Thomas Lewis) in 1906 and Lord Rhondda (David Alfred Thomas) in 1916 - early recognitions of Cardiff's dependence on coal.

# CARDIFF AND THE ARTS AND ENTERTAINMENT

Cardiff is justly proud of its many achievements in the arts and entertainment and of the impressive range of individuals from the city who have gained national and international reputations in the musical and literary world and in dramatic roles on stage and screen.

The city is, of course, the home of a major European opera company founded in 1946, Welsh National Opera with its own orchestra and famed chorus. The BBC National Orchestra of Wales is recognised as one of the UK's leading symphony orchestras and now Cardiff has the startling design of the Wales Millennium Centre in Cardiff Bay, with a 1,900 seat auditorium to stage the most ambitious productions over a wide range of artistic endeavours from opera and ballet to West End musicals. St David's Hall, opened in 1982 with just under 2,000 seats, is another fine venue for concerts, praised for its acoustics.

## Competitions and Festivals

The biennial BBC Singer of the World in Cardiff competition has become widely known as an international showcase for new operatic and concert talent since it was launched in 1983 and has a top prize of £10,000. Among the winners have been singers from Australia, China, Finland, Romania, Russia and the USA. The city also hosts the annual Worldport Festival, the Cardiff Screen Festival and the summer Cardiff Proms.

Cardiff is home to the highly regarded Royal Welsh College of Music and Drama which includes the Anthony Hopkins Centre, named after the College's most eminent former student. Chapter Arts Centre in Canton is a major European arts complex with two cinemas, three theatres, exhibition spaces and studios, while the Sherman Theatre opened in 1973 regularly stages performances of newly commissioned plays with an emphasis on youth theatre.

Cardiff as the capital of a bilingual country has frequent Welsh language events and is the base of the Welsh language television channel S4C. The largest annual Welsh language festival, the Royal National Eisteddfod of Wales is to be held in Cardiff in 2008 - its sixth visit to the city. Cardiff is also the home of the Welsh language youth movement, Urdd Gobaith Cymru, whose headquarters are in the Wales Millennium Centre where there are 150 residential places for young people. The Urdd National Eisteddfod is being held in Cardiff in 2005.

In 2004 the first biennial Cardiff Artes Mundi, the Welsh International Visual Arts Prize, was awarded. One of the most valuable prizes in the visual arts world it is worth £40,000 to its winner with a further £30,000 spent on purchases of the works of short-listed artists for the National Museums and Galleries of Wales. There were some 350 entries from 60 different countries for the first prize which was awarded to Xu Bing, a Chinese artist resident in New York.

Cardiff is one of the UK's major media centres with the studios of BBC and HTV as well as S4C and is a leader in the field of film animation. The International Animation Festival has been held in Cardiff on four occasions and animated films made in Cardiff have twice received Hollywood Oscar nominations.

### Arts Celebrities

Among the many leading arts personalities from Cardiff are the poets R.S. Thomas - who in 1996 was nominated for the Nobel Prize for Literature - Dannie Abse, Oliver Reynolds and Gillian Clarke, the writers Andrew Davies, Roald Dahl, Bernice Rubens, Ken Follett and Terry Nation (creator of the Daleks) while the composer of highly popular West End operettas, Ivor Novello, was a Cardiff man who also wrote *Keep The Homes Fires Burning* during World War One. The Hollywood film director Richard Marquand was from Cardiff and Marc Evans is another leading film director from the city. Cardiff-born Sir Howard

Stringer has held the top executive positions in New York with Sony and CBS.

Well-known actors from Cardiff include Ioan Gruffudd, Griff Rhys Jones, Angharad Rees, Andrew Howard and Matthew Rhys while two of its top singers are Dame Shirley Bassey and Charlotte Church. An earlier generation produced the popular singer and entertainer Tessie O'Shea, as well known on Broadway as in Britain.

Pop music has produced Huw Bumford and Guto Pryce of the Super Furry Animals and also Shakin' Stevens. The rock guitarist Dave Edmunds is from the city and another musician from Cardiff is Eos Chater of the classical girls quartet Bond,while the founder of the Brecon Jazz Festival was Cardiffian Jed Williams. The joint composer of the ever-popular *We'll Keep a Welcome* was Lyn Joshua from Cardiff.

**With a track record like this it is not surprising that in 2003 Cardiff was designated a UK Centre of Culture.**

# CARDIFF AND SPORT

Cardiff has a well established and enviable reputation for the staging of major sports events, as the birthplace of leading personalities across a wide range of sports and also for the quality of its sports and leisure facilities.

Cardiff's best known sports site is Cardiff Arms Park, now the location of the mighty Wales Millennium Stadium. It was completed in 1999 on what had once been muddy marshland reclaimed from the River Taff when the river was diverted to its present course in the early 1850s.

Since the first game was played there in 1874, Cardiff Arms Park has been the site of many memorable rugby and football matches, the Commonwealth Games track and field events in 1958 and the World Rugby Union finals of 1999. It has staged the FA Cup Final, the Carling Cup Final, the final of the Rugby League Challenge Cup and the European rugby union finals. British Speedway Championships are held there and it once had a greyhound track where the Welsh Greyhound Derby was run. The first ever women's rugby World Cup Final, won by the USA, was held there in 1991.

## A Variety of Venues

The Glamorgan County Cricket Club's ground at Sophia Gardens is a short walk from the Millennium Stadium. Glamorgan has won the county championship three times as well as the Sunday League championship twice while 16 Glamorgan players have been capped for England. There are ambitious plans to improve the ground to give it a capacity of 15,000 by 2009 in the hope that full Test matches might be played there. Sophia Gardens already hosts one day internationals.

Founded in 1899, Cardiff City of the First Division of the Football League has had its home at Ninian Park since 1910 but a new

30,000 capacity ground is intended to be built for the'Bluebirds' close to their old home. Cardiff City has the distinction of being the only club ever to take the FA Cup out of England when Arsenal were beaten 1-0 in 1927. Just two years before that Cardiff had reached the final only to lose to Sheffield United.

Also based in the city is the Cardiff Devils ice hockey side which has been a leading British team since its formation in 1986 winning the first Superleague title in 1997. It was the first British ice hockey side to qualify for a European competition. The Devils 2,500 seat ice rink in the city centre is intended to be replaced by a bigger arena in Cardiff Bay in the International Sports Village taking shape there.

Major boxing matches have been staged at the 5,500 seat Cardiff International Arena, at the ice rink and also at Cardiff Arms Park where in the world heavyweight title fight in 1993 Lennox Lewis beat Frank Bruno. The first world title fight ever staged in Wales was at Ninian Park in 1946 when Ronnie James of Pontardawe lost the lightweight contest in front of 40,000 spectators.

Baseball (not American baseball) is popular in Cardiff and also in Newport and international matches are staged regularly in the city between Wales and England where the game is centered on Liverpool.

Since 2000 Cardiff has been host to the four days of the Wales Rally of Great Britain, one of the 12 events in the annual series of rallies held across the world.

It was in Cardiff in 1905 that the International Bowling Board was founded and the city has had an indoor bowling stadium since 1960 while the first municipal bowling green was opened as early as 1905. The World Pool Championships have been held in the Cardiff International Arena as well as major snooker events like the Welsh Open Championship.

Leckwith Stadium for athletics, with a 5,500 seating capacity, was opened in 1989 and is to be replaced with a new stadium nearby to make way for Cardiff City's proposed new ground. The Welsh National Tennis Centre was opened on Ocean Way in 1995 and in 2002 the Wales National Indoor Arena for athletics was opened in Cyncoed. There are five 18-hole private golf clubs within Cardiff's boundaries and a public 9-hole course at Tongwynlais.

Cardiff is maintaining its reputation as one of Britain's leading sporting cities by the construction on an 80 acre (32 hectare) site of the Cardiff International Sports Village on the western side of Cardiff Bay. The first facility there is a 50 metre swimming pool with seating for 900 spectators. The lake at Cardiff Bay is the venue for yachting regattas, for powerboat racing and for the British universities windsurfing championships. Chinese dragon boat races are held regularly on the former Bute East Dock at Atlantic Wharf and since 2002 four kilometres of the River Taff between the city centre and the lake have been used for the Head of the Taff timed rowing events.

**Personalities**

Among the great number of leading sports personalities from Cardiff are footballers like John Toshack, Terry Yorath and Ryan Giggs and top class rugby union players like J.P.R. Williams, Terry Holmes and Gareth Llywellyn plus rugby league stars such as Jim Sullivan, Gus Risman and Billy Boston. The amazing Cardiff swimmer Paulo Radmilovich won gold medals in three Olympic Games in 1908, 1912 and 1920 and Irene Steer of Cardiff also won a swimming gold in 1912 while Cardiffian David Jacobs won a track relay gold that same year. Another Cardiff swimmer, Martyn Woodroffe, won a silver medal in the 1968 Olympics.

Top boxers produced by the city include champions like 'Peerless' Jim Driscoll, Jack Petersen, Joe Erskine, Nicky Piper, Steve Robinson and Barry Jones together with athletes of the calibre of Colin Jackson, Nigel Walker and Tanni Grey-Thompson as well as the winner of equestrian bronze medals in the Olympics of 1952 and 1960, David Broome, who was also the world showjumping champion in 1970.

**Tanni Grey-Thompson and Colin Jackson, both Olympic medal winners, were granted the Freedom of Cardiff in 2003 when they were described as 'superb ambassadors for the city'.**

## ONE HUNDRED CARDIFF PLACE NAMES EXPLAINED

**Adamsdown**  the name is that of a Scottish property owned by the Butes.

**Alexandra Gardens**  they are named after Queen Alexandra, the Danish wife of King Edward VII, who opened them in 1907.

**Andrews Arcade**  named after Solomon Andrews, a prominent nineteenth century Cardiff businessman.

**Arms Park**  named after the eighteenth century Cardiff Arms coaching inn which stood on the site of the present Angel Hotel and which was demolished in 1878. The park was a gift from the Butes. (The arms are the heraldic arms of Baron Cardiff, a Bute title).

**Beauchamp**  the castle's Beauchamp Tower is named after the Beauchamps, earls of Warwick, who began rebuilding the castle in the XVth century after the attack by Owain Glyndŵr in 1404.

**Bute Park**  the Scottish aristocratic family of the Butes dominated Cardiff for many years from the 1770s. This is one of the many names in the city serving as a reminder of their former influence. The family gave the parkland and the castle to Cardiff in 1947.

**Butetown**  the area of southern Cardiff roughly bounded by Callaghan Square to the north and Mountstuart Square to the south. Often known by its old nickname Tiger Bay, it does not cover the whole docks area.

| | |
|---|---|
| **Caerau** | the Welsh for forts. |
| **Callaghan Square** | named after Jim Callaghan (Lord Callaghan) long-serving Labour MP in Cardiff and Prime Minister from 1976-1979. |
| **Canton** | the settlement on the Canna, the name of a brook. |
| **Cardiff/Caerdydd** | the Welsh for fort on the Taff. |
| **Castell Coch** | the Welsh for red castle, rebuilt by the third Marquis of Bute in the 1870s and donated by the Bute family to the state in 1950. |
| **Cathays** | from an old English word hay or hai meaning hedge or enclosure - cat or cad may be from the Welsh for battle. |
| **Cefncarnau** | the Welsh for hillside or ridge of cairns. |
| **Cefnmably** | the Welsh for hillside or ridge of Mably(Mabli), a personal name. |
| **Cefn Onn** | the Welsh for ash tree hillside or ridge. |
| **Churchill Way** | named in honour of Sir Winston Churchill in 1949 after he had been made a Freeman of Cardiff in 1948. The road covers the Docks Feeder which tapped the River Taff to provide water for the Bute West Dock. |
| **Clarence Bridge** | named after the Duke of Clarence who opened the original bridge in 1890. The new bridge was opened in 1975. |

**Crockerton/
Crockherbtown**  an old English name for an area
where herbs (crocks) and vegeta-
bles were grown.

**Creigiau**  the Welsh for rocks or cliffs.

**Crwys**  the Welsh for cross, a reference to
the cross marking the northern
boundary of the old parish of St
John.

**Culverhouse Cross**  culverhouse is an old English term
for dovecot and the cross is the
place where the road from Cardiff to
Cowbridge met the road from St
Fagans to Wenvoe.

**Cyncoed**  the Welsh for main or early wood.

**Cyntwell**  the Welsh for a sanctuary or holy
place.

**Duke Street**  probably a corruption of Duck Street,
a part of the town where poulterers
traded.

**Dumballs**  flat, muddy moorland.

**Dumfries Place**  Earl of Dumfries was one of the titles
of the Marquis of Bute.

**Ely**  Elai in Welsh, the river name
possibly meaning slow moving.

**Fforest Fawr**  the Welsh for big forest.

**Fforest Ganol**  the Welsh for middle forest.

**Fitzhamon Embankment**  Robert Fitzhamon was the Norman
warlord who began the construction
of Cardiff Castle.

**Gabalfa**  the Welsh for a place for ferry boats
to cross the river (Taff).

**Glantaf**  the Welsh for Taff bank.

**Golate**  gole or golet is an old French term
for a narrow stream or gutter of water.

| | |
|---|---|
| **Greyfriars** | the site of the medieval friary established by the Franciscans whose habit was grey. |
| **Gwaelod-y-garth** | the Welsh for bottom of the garth, garth meaning hill or headland. |
| **Hamadryad** | the name of an old sailing ship brought to Cardiff in 1860 and used as a permanent seamen's hospital. It was broken up in 1905 and replaced by the Hamadryad Hospital, closed in 2002. |
| **Heol Hir** | the Welsh for long road. |
| **Herbert Street/Tower** | the Herberts, Earls of Pembroke, dominated Cardiff from the sixteenth century to the eighteenth century. |
| **Ifor Bach, Clwb** | named in honour of Ifor Bach (Ifor ap Meurig), the Welsh Lord of Senghenydd in the twelfth century and considered a local hero. |
| **Insole** | Insole Court was the home of the Insoles who were prominent South Wales coal owners. |
| **Lamby** | a Norse word meaning long dwelling. (See Womanby). |
| **Leckwith** | Llechwedd in Welsh, meaning the hillside on the west bank of the River Ely. |
| **Lisvane** | Llysfaen in Welsh meaning stone court. |
| **Llandaff/Llandaf** | the Welsh for church on the Taff. |
| **Llanedeyrn** | St Edeyrn's Church. |
| **Llanishen/Llanisien** | St Isien's Church. |
| **Llanrumney/Llanrhymni** | Church on the Rumney (river). |

**Lloyd George Avenue** named after David Lloyd George, the only Welshman to date to have been Prime Minister of the UK (1916-1922).

**Loudon Square** named after Flora, Countess of Loudon, mother-in-law of the second Marquis of Bute.

**Mackintosh Place** named after the Scottish landowning family, who had extensive properties in Cardiff.

**Maes-y-coed Road** the Welsh for wood field.

**Maindy/Maendy** the Welsh for stone house.

**Melingriffith** melin is Welsh for mill so it means Griffith's mill.

**Mountstuart** the name of the Bute's family home on the Isle of Bute.

**Mynachdy** the Welsh name for monastery - the land here once belonged to the Cistercian white monks of Llantarnam Abbey near Caerleon.

**Newtown** the area centered on Jury's Hotel and the Cardiff International Arena was once home to thousands of Irish immigrants and was known as 'little Ireland'.

**Ninian Park** named after Lord Ninian Crichton Stuart, second son of the third Marquis of Bute and whose elder brother John gave the land to Cardiff City. Ninian was killed in 1915 on the Western Front five years after the football ground was opened.

**Pantbach** the Welsh for little hollow or valley.

**Pantmawr** the Welsh for big hollow or valley.

**Pencoed** the Welsh for top of the wood.

**Pengam** the Welsh for crooked top.

**Pentrebane**     pentre here is not the Welsh for village but a distorted form of cefn, a ridge, and bane is a personal name.

**Pentwyn**     the Welsh for mound top.

**Pentyrch**     the Welsh for top of the burrow.

**Penylan**     the Welsh for the top of a hillside or bank.

**Pontcanna**     the Welsh for bridge over the Canna - the name of a brook.

**Pontprennau**     the Welsh for wooden bridge.

**Plas Mawr**     the Welsh for big mansion.

**Plas Newydd**     the Welsh for new mansion.

**Pwll Mawr**     the Welsh for big pit or pond.

**Radyr /Radur**     from the Latin oratorium, a prayer house or oratory chapel usually for private worship.

**Roath**     Y Rath in Welsh - a fort or fortified place. (Roath Court once had a protective ditch).

**Rhiwbina /Rhiwbeina**     the Welsh for the slope or hillside of beina - possibly a personal name. (The place name is known from the eleventh century).

**Rhydlafar**     the Welsh for ford on the Lafar, a stream name.

**Rhydypennau**     the Welsh for cattle ford - pennau referring to heads of cattle.

**Rumney**     Rhymni in Welsh, the river name which may mean a boring river from the Welsh word rhwmp meaning gimlet.

**St Andrew's Crescent**     named after the Scottish patron saint whose church was here but is now Eglwys Dewi Sant, dedicated to the Welsh patron saint, David.

**Sherman Theatre**     built through the generosity— of the Sherman brothers Abe and Harry of Cardiff's Sherman Football Pools.

**Sophia Gardens**     named after Lady Sophia, Marchioness of Bute, second wife of the second Marquis of Bute. This was Cardiff's first public park opened in 1858 and probably the earliest urban public park in Wales

**Splott**     Y sblot in Welsh - a farm name. It was part of the estate of the Bishop of Llandaff so it may be derived from 'God's plot'.

**Taff/Taf**     the river name which probably means dark coloured.

**Temperance Town**     once the name of the area around South Gate House and the Central Bus Station where there had been a Temperance Hall.

**The Hayes/Yr Aes**     from an old English word meaning hedge or enclosure - this was originally an area of small gardens.

**The Marl**     an area of rich lime soil.

**Thompson's Park**     named after the Thompson family, former owners of the Spillers flour company, who gave the park to the city in 1924.

**Tiger Bay**     its origin is uncertain, possibly from a popular song of the 1870s applied to Butetown.(In the early nineteenth century 'tiger' was slang for a smartly liveried boy groom and later, by extension, was applied to colourfully dressed persons).

| | |
|---|---|
| **Tongwynlais** | the Welsh for unploughed (ley) land by the white brook. |
| **Tredegarville** | the area between Newport Road and Richmond Road which once belonged to the Morgan family of Tredegar House, Newport. |
| **Trelai** | the Welsh for settlement on the River Ely (Elai). |
| **Tremorfa** | the Welsh for settlement by the sea marsh. |
| **Tynant** | the Welsh for house by the stream. |
| **Velindre** | Felindre in Welsh meaning mill place. |
| **Victoria Park** | opened in 1897 to mark Queen Victoria's Diamond Jubilee. |
| **Wenallt** | the Welsh for fair hillside. |
| **Wentloog** | the Anglicised form of the Welsh Gwynllŵg, a personal name. |
| **Wern Goch** | the Welsh for red marsh. |
| **Windsor Place/ Esplanade** | the Windsors were the family who owned Cardiff Castle before the Butes. |
| **Womanby Street** | this is likely to be a corruption of 'hundemanby', a Norse word meaning huntsman's dwelling. (See Lamby). |
| **Working Street** | this is possibly derived from a term for little marsh or little wasteland. |

# CARDIFF'S GROWTH

•

**Before becoming a city -**
Cardiff consisted of the original small medieval
borough to the south of the castle plus Adamsdown,
Butetown, Canton, Cathays, Grangetown, Leckwith,
Plasnewydd, Roath and Splott.

•

**After becoming a city -**
Cardiff's boundaries were extended between 1922
and 1951 to include Caerau, Cyncoed, Ely,
Fairwater, Gabalfa, Heath, Llandaff, Llanishen,
Llanrumney, Pentrebane and Rumney.

•

**Since becoming the Welsh capital -**
Cardiff has expanded to include Coryton, Creigiau,
Gwaelod-y-garth, Lisvane, Llanedeyrn,
Michelston-super-Ely, Morganstown, Pentwyn,
Pentyrch, Pontprennau, Radyr, Rhiwbina,
St Fagans, St. Mellons, Tongwynlais, Trowbridge
and Whitchurch.

•

# FIFTY FACTS ABOUT CARDIFF

1. Although there was a Roman fort at Cardiff for some 350 years, the Roman name for Cardiff is not known but many other Roman place names in Wales have been recorded.
2. The small church which was to become Llandaff Cathedral was founded about 560 AD during the lifetime of St David, the patron saint of Wales.
3. William the Conqueror passed through Cardiff in 1081 on a pilgrimage to St David's and probably gave orders for the castle to be built.
4. The Conqueror's eldest son Robert, Duke of Normandy, died in Cardiff Castle where he had been kept a prisoner for eight years before his death in 1134 following a family dispute about the division of William the Conqueror's lands.
5. Geoffrey of Monmouth, whose book *The History of the Kings of Britain* which appeared in 1136 and popularised the legends of King Arthur, was made archdeacon of Llandaff in 1147 and may have died there in 1155.
6. There was once a medieval leper hospital, St Mary Magdalene, outside the medieval town walls in modern Queen Street near where the Thistle Hotel now stands.
7. Common criminals were hanged at Gallows Field, near the junction of City Road and Crwys Road, where there were four gibbets.
8. William Morgan, translator of the Bible into Welsh in 1588, was Bishop of Llandaff from 1595 to 1601.
9. The medieval walled town of Cardiff, wholly on the eastern side of the River Taff, had a smaller area, some 17 hectares (42 acres), than today's Civic Centre which is about 28 hectares (60 acres).
10. Reputedly, the famous buccaneer Sir Henry Morgan was born in Llanrumney about 1635.
11. After a week long visit to Cardiff by Charles I in 1645 during the Civil War, there was no further visit by a reigning monarch to Cardiff until Edward VII's arrival in 1907.

12. The last major battle ever fought in Wales was at St Fagans in 1648 when the Parliamentary New Model Army defeated the Royalists. Of some 11,000 men involved about 200 were killed.

13. A small part of Cardiff's medieval town wall, which was one mile (1.6 kilometres) long and some 12 feet (4 metres) high, is still standing opposite Northgate House in Kingsway.

14. There were once coal mines and iron ore mines inside Cardiff's present boundaries at Gwaelod-y-garth, Pentyrch and Fforest Fawr near Tongwynlais.

15. Bob Hope's parents, Harry and Avis, were married in Cardiff in 1891.

16. The world's first radio message transmitted across water was by Guglielmo Marconi in May 1897, from Flat Holm to Lavernock Point.

17. In 1896 the first news event ever filmed anywhere in Britain showed the Prince and Princess of Wales arriving at the Cardiff Exhibition of that year.

18. In 1884 the acquital of Dr William Price in a Cardiff trial on a charge of cremating the body of his infant son, had the effect of making cremation legal throughout Britain.

19. E.T. Willows, the Cardiff airship pioneer, in 1910 became the first man to fly an airship across the English Channel from England to France.

20. The first scheduled night flights anywhere in Britain were made in 1938 from Cardiff Airport, then at Pengam, to Weston-super-Mare.

21. The Cardiff-born pilot Griffith James (Taffy) Powell, held the trans-Atlantic flight record from 1937 to 1944 taking 10 hours 22 minutes to fly from Newfoundland to Ireland. Another Cardiff-born pilot, Sir Arthur Brown, set a further record in 1955 taking just 6 hours 32 minutes to fly from Ottawa to London.

22. The world's first scheduled helicopter service was established between Cardiff, Wrexham and Liverpool in 1950.

23. The Royal National Eisteddfod of Wales has been held in Cardiff five times between 1883 and 1978.

24. Some 16 per cent of Cardiff's population have one or more skills in the Welsh language according to the 2001 census.

25. The first local Welsh language community newspaper (papur bro) in Wales, *Y Dinesydd*, was launched in Cardiff in 1973 and is still being published.

26. Cardiff has had a Catholic Archbishop since 1916.

27. Pope John Paul II made the first ever papal visit to Wales on an official trip to Cardiff in 1982.

28. The first purpose-built mosque in Cardiff was opened in 1947 and Britain's first ever Muslim conference took place in the city in 1949.

29. About eight per cent of Cardiff's population belong to ethnic minorities.

30. Cardiff has a full time university student population of some 25,000.

31. Cardiff is one of 11 places in the UK, and the only one in Wales, where royal gun salutes can be fired.

32. In 1917 during World War One (1914-1918) the Angel Hotel was taken over by the United States Navy and renamed USS *Chattinouka.*

33. During World War Two (1939-1945) 345 people were killed in air raids on Cardiff, about 500 were seriously injured, nearly 30,000 premises were damaged and 600 demolished.

34. Of all British cathedrals, only Coventry Cathedral sustained more bomb damage than Llandaff Cathedral during World War Two.

35. In 1976 James Callaghan (later Lord Callaghan of Cardiff) became the first MP representing a Cardiff constituency to become Prime Minister.

36. In 1976 George Thomas (later Viscount Tonypandy) became the first MP representing a Cardiff constituency to become Speaker of the House of Commons.

37. One of the regular six monthly European Summit Meetings of the heads of the (then) 15 member states of the European Union took place in Cardiff over two days in June 1998.

38. Cardiff Bay lake 500 acres (200 hectares) in area is the largest fresh water lake in South Wales.

39. Cardiff's Equitation Centre at Pontcanna was Britain's first municipally-owned riding centre when it opened in 1970.

40. Cardiff's Wales Millennium Stadium is the largest stadium in Europe with a retractable roof and the only such stadium in the British Isles.

41. Cardiff City in 1927 became the first non-English side to win the FA Cup and the FA Cup Final was played for the first time outside England in Cardiff in 2001.

42. The animated films *Famous Fred* and *The Canterbury Tales*, largely made in Cardiff, both received Hollywood Oscar nominations in 1998 and 2000 respectively.

43. In 1981 the Women's Peace March, which led to the establishment of the Greenham Common Peace Camp, began at Cardiff's City Hall.

44. Reputedly, it was in Cardiff Coal Exchange in 1907 that Britain's first £1 million cheque was signed - for a sale of coal to the United States Navy.

45. Cardiff is one of the flattest cities in the British Isles and considerable areas of the south are built on land reclaimed from the sea since the 1830s.

46. Ten per cent of Cardiff's area is public parkland.

47. The highest temperature ever recorded in Cardiff was 32.6°C (93°F) on 29 July 1911 and the lowest temperature ever recorded was -15°C (5°F) on 21 January 1940.

48. Two of Cardiff's three rivers, the Taff and the Rumney, have their sources in the Brecon Beacons National Park and the third, the Ely, has its source in the Rhondda Valley. Because of the construction of the barrage in Cardiff Bay, the Ely and the Taff are no longer tidal rivers.

49. The huge tidal range of the Bristol Channel, the second largest in the world after the Bay of Fundy in Canada, means that shipping can only enter and leave Cardiff docks for about two hours either side of the two daily high tides. (Spring tides can be as high as 42 to 44 feet - about 13 metres).

50. Cardiff was the first British city to make a twinning agreement with any Chinese city - Xiamen (formerly called Amoy). Cardiff is also twinned with Baltimore County, Maryland (USA), Hordaland County (Norway), Lugansk (Ukraine), Nantes (France) and Stuttgart (Germany).

*The Bute Docks in the late 19th century with Cardiff already one of the world's busiest ports. Queen Alexandra Dock is yet to be opened.*

*The docks in 1929 with decline setting in.*

*The docks shortly before Cardiff was made capital in 1955, with all five docks operating. The barrage is still 50 years in the future.*

*The Civic Centre, built over 90 years, its oldest building the University of Wales Registry opened in 1903 two years before Cardiff became a city.*

# CARDIFF OBSERVED
## Fifty Comments on the City

'At that time the castle of Caerdyff was surrounded with high walls guarded by one hundred and twenty men-at-arms, a numerous body of archers, and a strong watch. The city also contained many stipendiary soldiers.'
**Gerald of Wales after visiting Cardiff in 1188, describing the abduction of the Earl and Countess of Gloucester from the castle by Ifor Bach, Lord of Senghenydd in 1158.**

'The town of Cardiff is well walled and is by estimation a mile in compass ... In the walls be five gates. The castle is a great thing and is strong but now in some ruin. There be two parish churches in the town.'
**John Leland, antiquary, 1552.**

'Cardiff is the general resort of pirates and there they are sheltered and protected.'
**A local Justice of the Peace, 1577.**

'The castle contains luxurious apartments and attractive gardens with many fair houses and large streets in the town ...the chieftest town of Glamorgan ... the river Taff runneth near the town walls in the west part of the town ...'
**Rice Merrick (Rhys Meurig), Glamorgan historian,1580.**

'The River Taff, sliding down from the Hills, runneth towards the Sea ... to Cardiff, a proper fine Town (as Townes go in this Country) and a very commodious Harbour.'
**William Camden, 1585.**

'The fayrest town in Wales, yett not the wealthiest.'
**George Owen, Pembrokeshire historian, 1602.**

'The fairest town in all of South Wales, with its castle in good repair, town walls and a quay.'
**John Speed, mapmaker, 1610.**

'I preached ... in the court-house in Cardiff ... the hearers here were more than for many years to give hope that even in this desolate town, God may build up the waste places.'
**John Wesley, 1767.**

Cardiff '... appeared with more of the furniture of antiquity about it than any other town we had seen in Wales.'
**William Gilpin, 1770.**

'We have no coal exported from this port, nor ever shall, as it would be too expensive to bring it down here from the interior part of the country.'
**A customs officer, 1782.**

'The ivy around the old tower and in the keep is cut down, the sides of which are sloped, and mowed: not a tree is planted ... so altogether it seems to me as only calculated for the town bowling green.'
**John Byng, 1787, on Lancelot (Capability) Brown's landscaping of Cardiff Castle in the 1770s.**

'The canal ... is completed and a fleet of canal boats have arrived in Cardiff... to the great joy of the whole town.'
**The opening of the Glamorganshire Canal between Merthyr Tydfil and Cardiff, February 1794.**

Cardiff '... by 1821, when it had a population of three and a half thousand, ranked only twenty-seventh among the towns of Wales, smaller than Llanelli and Pembroke let alone Merthyr Tydfil. It was still largely unpaved and unlighted and

its sanitation little better than 1750 when a woman drowned after falling into a privy at the King David Inn.'
**Gareth Williams, *1905 And All That,* 1996.**

'... instead of the quiet of 30 years ago, an eternal racket has succeeded it this (summer) season, every bed of the Inn (The Cardiff Arms) being filled and many travellers obliged to go on with tired horses.'
**A traveller to Cardiff, 1830.**

'A direful swamp over which the spring tides flowed, leaving dangerous dykes, swamps and gullies.'
**A description of the East Moors in the mid 1830s before the Bute West Dock was built there between 1837 and 1839.**

'There are several courts, alleys and lanes behind the principal streets, occupied by families bordering on pauperdom ... although the town is certainly thriving and likely to continually improve.'
**Royal Commission on local government, 1837**.

'Nothing can be worse than the house accommodation for ... the poor in this town; the overcrowding is fearful, beyond anything of the kind I have ever known of .'
**T.W. Rammell, *Report on the Sanitary Conditions of the Town of Cardiff,* 1850.**

Quay Street '... now bears few traces of its former stir and bustle by the rough tars and plodding fishermen who used to navigate their craft to the Old Quay, and the patois and swagger of the sailors and fishermen have long since been exchanged for the jargon and shouts of the Welsh and Hereford drovers in the street nearby for with the shifting

course of enterprise, the town has a new scene for the marine population who now sail through the Dock and the Canal banks.'
**A contemporary description of Cardiff, 1858.**

'The charm of an ancient and impressive rite was destroyed by the screech of railway locomotives on the one side and by the hideous noise of a show ground on the other.'
**A description of the Gorsedd ceremony held alongside the Taff Vale Railway shed at the Cardiff National Eisteddfod of Wales, 1883.**

'Cardiff is singularly deficient in places of innocent recreative resort, though it is full of moral reformers.'
**Welsh ministers conference, 1895.**

'... the Taff Vale's station in the principal street of Cardiff ... had most of the architectural features of a moderately glorified fowl-house. It is only fair to add that in time, improvements were made.'
**E.L. Ehrons, *Locomotive and Train Working in the latter part of the 19th century,* 1953**

'Castell Coch is quite simply one of the most romantic, if unexpected buildings in Wales ... in 1871 Lord Bute asked (William) Burges to carry out a survey and make proposals... Work began in 1875 and the framework was finished by 1879 ... it took a further ten years to complete the interior decoration and fittings. The resulting castle is a decorative extravaganza ... Always there is something else to see at once both surprising and captivating.'
**David M. Robinson and Roger S. Thomas *Welsh Castles and Historic Places,* 1990.**

'Presiding over this world in its imperial days (the early twentieth century) sucking it dry of talent and wealth, was the noble and squalid city of Cardiff ... catching the town-planning fever and acquiring the huge Bute estate ... to raise the baroque palaces of its bourgeoisie, to balance the merchant palazzi clustering around that huge and ponderous ideology in Bath stone, its Coal Exchange ... this was the artery of empire and the jugular vein of capitalist Wales within which every other Wales had to live.'

**Gwyn A. Williams, *When Was Wales ?*, 1985.**

'It is no great arrogance on the part of this great town to be ambitious, to exert itself to serve the interests of the Welsh people to such an extent as to deserve the .title of Metropolis of Wales.'

***Cardiff Times*, April 1905**

'We were welcomed by the Lord Mayor and were greeted outside the station by the largest crowd we have yet to meet ... the greeting to Wales will live long in the memory of every member of the team.'

**George Dixon, manager of the first New Zealand All Blacks on their arrival in Cardiff, December 1905.**

'There is no more interesting study in town growth than Cardiff. At the census of 1851 it was a place of some 20,000 inhabitants with no influence and no reputation. Now it is one of the most thriving cities in the country, a centre of trade and commerce and a great port. In every respect, the growth has been remarkable.'

**Board of Trade report, 1908.**

'... from 1841 downwards the population of Cardiff has increased 10,000 ... for every additional million tons of coal shipped from its port ... to use a colloquialism, 'Coal is King' '.

**Enquiry into Industrial Unrest in South Wales, 1917.**

'Cardiff is as much an English as a Welsh city, a mongrel border town in which the Welsh strain has been so diluted as to produce a far more variegated social pattern than I was accustomed to (in Aberystwyth).'

**Goronwy Rees in *A Chapter of Accidents*, 1972 on adolescence in Cardiff in 1920.**

'Cardiff is not in Wales, Cardiff is merely a cosmopolitan village about 40 miles to the east of us.'

**T.J. Rees, Director of Education, Swansea, January 1938.**

'Puff, little engine, to the valleys at daybreak,
To northward and westward with a voice in the dawn,
And shout to the people that prosperity's coming,
And that coal can be changed into ingots of gold,
And that Cardiff shall be famous when the sun goes down.'

***Dawn* by Idris Davies (1905-1953).**

'The local newspapers of the early 1920s were full of reports of the bankruptcy of many of Cardiff's newer shipowners, who found themselves facing ruin as they were forced to sell off their vessels for a sixth of the price they had paid for them ... It was a blow from which Cardiff, both as a port and a shipowning centre, never recovered.'

**J. Geraint Jenkins and David Jenkins,
*Cardiff Shipowners,* 1986.**

'The Civic Centre of the city, accessible yet in pleasant open surroundings, is the finest in the whole kingdom. Here in Cathays Park is a group of fine modern buildings that serve almost every civilised need'.

**H.L.V. Fletcher, *South Wales*, 1956.**

In 1955 '... Cardiff was declared to be the capital of Wales after a contest with Caernarfon in the north and Aberystwyth in the mid-west. To some extent the contest highlighted the divisions

within Wales but the good natured acceptance of the decision indicated that the postwar heightening of Welsh consciousness was at last beginning to unite the principality. The old petty adage of the north - better no capital at all than Cardiff - had disappeared.'
**Richard Weight, *Patriots*, 2002.**

'That city (Cardiff) received the greatest stimulus from the growth of industry and mining. Accordingly to Cardiff have been attracted most of the head offices of commercial and government concerns in Wales. Without doubt it is the de facto economic capital of Wales.'
**J. Gareth Thomas and Harold Carter, *Wales*, 1957**

'... Cardiff, to all but a few Welshmen, is the city. One half of Cardiff is the life that streams into it from the northern hills. For millions of children from the Rhondda Cardiff has been the nerve-end of all delight, the glare at the end of the tunnel, their first contact with a well-lit urbanity, the first visible evidence of wealth and ease.'
**Gwyn Thomas, *A Welsh Eye*, 1964.**

'Cardiff is obviously memorable ...
In Victorian Britain there is nothing to match its obsessive exoticism ... Cardiff is an urban dream - or rather a dream castle in a city ... as such it is incomparable.'
**J.Mordaunt Crook, *William Burges and the High Victorian Dream*, 1981.**

'Cardiff has one area unique among British towns which is undeniably grand and which contributes a very great deal to its identity as the capital of Wales. The Civic Centre in Cathays Park is one of the most remarkable collections of Edwardian public buildings to be found in the British Isles.'
**Ken Powell, *Country Life*, January 1982.**

'... in any part of West Wales being trounced by Cardiff
(at rugby) is bad news. Nobody west of Bridgend
cares for Cardiff.'
**John Morgan, journalist and broadcaster, 1985.**

'... behind the respectable temples of local government and
the warrens of bureaucracy, the smart stores, big hotels and
flash restaurants, there is an element of the seedy about
Cardiff, and where there is seediness, there are usually
'characters' who can be raw material for a writer.'
**John Tripp (1927-1986), Cardiff poet.**

'Where will you spend eternity ?
The posters question us.
The answer comes quite readily:
Waiting for a Cardiff bus.'
**Harry Webb (1920-1994).**

'Tiger Bay was Cardiff's Dodge City when the town
was soaring on the dizzy thermals of the coal boom and
the riches of the valleys were pouring in ... Cardiff became
the greatest coal port in the world and some of its tycoons
made handsome fortunes ... Cardiff was the natural choice
for a capital and the granting of the status was a
recognition of Wales and the Welsh nation ... It has
cleaned the coal dust from its fingernails and has become
a major business and administrative centre.'
**Trevor Fishlock, *Wales and the Welsh*, 1972.**

'When I arrived in Cardiff ... my first impression was of a
garden city rather than a capital. Where else do you reach
the town centre through miles of parkland ?'
**Peter Sagar, *Wales*, 1985 (German), 1991 (English).**

'Cardiff is an exciting city that is still developing, and unlike Edinburgh or London, which rest on their wistful and long histories, Cardiff pushes on, as one of Europe's largest regeneration projects transforms the old dock lands...'
**Mike Parker and Paul Whitfield,**
***Wales: The Rough Guide*, 1994.**

'Being near the border with England gave Cardiff a rather ambiguous character ... Few people spoke Welsh and those that did were considered eccentric. The people were deeply hospitable and Cardiff was good to us. I will always love it for the warmth with which it took us in.'
**Bernice Rubens, prize winning novelist and daughter of Russian Jewish immigrants, on growing up in Cardiff, 1997.**

'Next week Cardiff is the host city for the final summit of Britain's EU presidency. The choice of the Welsh capital is a fitting acknowledgement of the city's recent renaissance and the principality's broader resurgence.'
***The Times*, 13 June 1998.**

'Hardly more than a village at the start of the nineteenth century, and thus accustomed to rapid change, the city looks forward to an increasingly dynamic role ... Its role as the capital of the principality ... reinforced by the presence of the Welsh Assembly.'
***Wales: The Michelin Guide*, 1999.**

'Britain's latest and greatest sporting wonder will be unveiled when the Millennium Stadium in Cardiff plays host to its first event on Saturday. It is an outrageously confident architectural statement ... this impressively realised vision stands in the middle of the capital city of Wales.'
***The Times*, 19 June 1999.**

'The great thing about Cardiff is that it has managed to sustain its energy and vibrancy. Word has spread that it's worth a visit, so much so that it's now a staple destination for those visiting the UK.'
**Mel Cooper, *The Britain Guide*, Lonely Planet, 2003.**

'The Wales Millennium Centre is that rare thing in Britain: a viable public building project snatched from the jaws of fiasco ... the building itself looks immense; an imposing mound of Welsh slate, Welsh spruce wood, Welsh glass and Welsh steel ... rising beside redeveloped Cardiff Bay.'
**Richard Morrison, *The Times,* 15 December 2003.**

'Cardiff is a confident city - small enough to remain friendly but big enough not to be boring. Only the capital since 1955, it's been surging into its status as if on fast-forward ... Cardiff has more green space per resident than any other city in Europe.'
**Abigail Hole, Etain O'Caroll and John King, *Wales*, Lonely Planet, 2004.**

## EVENTS ELSEWHERE IN 1905
## AS CARDIFF BECAME A CITY

### W A L E S

It was an appalling year for mining tragedies in the South Wales coalfield. In July at the National No.2 Colliery, Wattstown in the Rhondda, an explosion killed 119 miners while in an earlier explosion in March, also in the Rhondda, 33 miners were killed at the Cambrian Colliery, Clydach Vale. In January 11 men lost their lives in an explosion at Elba Colliery, Gowerton, seven men were killed sinking a shaft at Nine Mile Point, Cwmfelinfach near Cross Keys in July and three miners were killed in a roof fall at Ladysmith Colliery, Glynneath in June.

This was the second and final year of the last great religious revival to sweep through Wales led by Evan Roberts of Loughor, Carmarthenshire. The National Eisteddfod of Wales was held at Mountain Ash but no one was judged good enough to earn the Chair. The actor and playwright Emlyn Williams was born in Mostyn, the poet Idris Davies was born in Rhymney, the popular actress Rachel Thomas was born in Alltwen, Swansea, and the distinguished writer Glyn Jones was born in Merthyr Tydfil. Arthur Edwin Stevens, inventor of the world's first wearable hearing aid, was born in Monmouth and Cyril Frederick Walters, the first Welshman to captain an England Test side (against Australia in 1934) was born in Bedlinog, Merthyr Tydfil. Also in Merthyr Tydfil, which was made a borough this year, the first Labour Party mayor in Wales, Enoch Morrell, was elected.

The University of Wales awarded its first degrees in music and the famous diva Adelina Patti, then living at Craig-y-nos Castle in the Swansea Valley, made her first recordings.

The deaths occurred of the socialist and nationalist poet Robert Jones Derfel of Llandderfel, Gwynedd, and of the pioneer photographer John Thomas of Cellan, Cardiganshire.

Wales won its fourth rugby union Triple Crown and Wrexham won football's Welsh Cup for the sixth time.

## BRITAIN AND IRELAND

David Lloyd George first entered the Liberal cabinet as President of the Board of Trade and the Scotsman Sir Henry Campbell-Bannerman became Prime Minister. In London the Automobile Association was established and in Dublin Arthur Griffith founded Sinn Fein. In the campaign for votes for women, the first two militant suffragettes were imprisoned.

The death occurred of Thomas Bernardo, Irish-born founder of the children's homes, and also of the great actor Sir Henry Irving who had appeared at Cardiff's Theatre Royal the previous year on his farewell tour. Four leading British actors Robert Donat, Leo Genn, James Robertson Justice and Robert Newton were born and the year also saw the birth of the composer Sir Michael Tippett. Elgar's Introduction and Allegro Pomp and Circumstance March No.2 was first performed and Puccini's *Madame Butterfly* had its British premiere at Covent Garden.

The FA Cup Final, played at Crystal Palace, was won by Aston Villa and the finals of the first known British beauty contest were held at Newcastle-upon-Tyne. Sir Arthur Conan Doyle's *The Return of Sherlock Holmes* and H.G.Wells' *Kipps* were published.

## THE WORLD

Russia was in turmoil: in January some 500 people were killed at a demonstration in St Petersburg on 'Bloody Sunday' and in June sailors aboard the battleship *Potemkin* at Odessa on the Black Sea mutinied and threw some officers overboard. In August eight of the mutineers were executed. In Warsaw in May, 500 demonstrators against Russian rule in Poland were shot and again in Odessa an estimated 6,000 demonstrators were killed while also in the same city over 1,000 Jews were killed during a pogrom. In Chile 500 people were killed in political demonstrations, in Athens the Greek Prime Minister was assassinated and in Turkey hundreds of Armenians were massacred. Russia was forced to concede victory to Japan in the war between them which had begun in 1904.

In the USA the Wright Brothers developed their Flyer III, the first fully practical powered aeroplane which could fly in circles and figures of eight while staying airborne for over half an hour. Also in the USA the first Rotary Club was founded in Chicago, in Pittsburg the world's first purpose-built cinema was opened and in New York pizzas went on sale introduced by the city's Italian community. Again in New York the Gramophone Company first used the *His Master's Voice* painting in its advertising.

Some 10,000 people died in an earthquake in Lahore, India, while Norway achieved independence from Sweden amicably and Alberta and Saskatchewan became provinces of Canada. In South Africa the Cullinan diamond, over 1¼ pounds in weight, was found at Pretoria. The Trans-Siberian Railway was officially opened with journeys from Paris to Vladivostok via Moscow taking 21 days.

The year saw the births of the writers Jean-Paul Sartre and Arthur Koestler, the trombonist and band leader Tommy Dorsey, Christian Dior the French fashion designer and a number of future Hollywood stars - Claudette Colbert, Henry Fonda, Greta Garbo, Myrna Loy, Joel McRea and Franchot Tone. The eccentric billionaire industrialist and Hollywood film producer Howard Hughes was born in the USA and in Germany the Nazi Party leader Albert Speer and the heavyweight boxer Max Schmeling were born. In New Zealand the great All Blacks player George Nepia was born.

The French science fiction writer Jules Verne died and Baroness Orczy published her best selling novel *The Scarlet Pimpernel*. The long-lasting incandescent electric light bulb went on sale, Albert Einstein published his General Theory of Relativity, and in Switzerland the Simplon rail tunnel was opened, at 12½ miles (20 kilometres) the world's longest at the time. Franz

Lehar's highly popular operetta *The Merry Widow* was first performed, and the Nobel Prize for Medicine and Physics was won by Heinrich Koch for his work on tuberculosis (TB), a particularly deadly scourge in Wales.

Thomas Pryce from Brymbo, Wrexham, became the first Labour Prime Minister of South Australia.

## W A L E S

In November an excursion train from Treberbert, Rhondda, to London derailed in Bedfordshire and ten passengers were killed. The Farmers' Union of Wales was founded in Aberystwyth, the Neath River Bridge at Briton Ferry was opened and Luciano Pavarotti made his first stage appearance outside Italy as a member of his father's choir from Modena competing at the Llangollen International Musical Eisteddfod. Welsh National Opera staged its first production in London, Verdi's *Nabucco.*

In the general election which was won by the Conservatives, Wales returned 27 Labour MPs, five Conservative, three Liberals and one Liberal-Conservative. The once powerful Monmouthshire and South Wales Coal Owners' Association was dissolved, July unemployment in Wales was 13,400 - the lowest peace-time figure ever recorded - and Rhondda was made a borough.

Six miners were killed in an explosion at Blaenhirwaun Colliery, Cross Hands, in September and the deaths also occurred of Thomas Jones, founder of the adult education centre Coleg Harlech, of Percy Bush the legendary Welsh rugby international, and of the Briton Ferry-born popular song writer Harry Parr-Davies who had written songs for stars like Gracie Fields and George Formby. Will John, former Labour MP in the Rhondda and miners' leader there who had been imprisoned for his alleged part in the Tonypandy Riots of 1910-1911, also died this year.

The first national nature reserve in Wales, Cwm Idwal in Snowdonia, was designated and also in Snowdonia the Plas-y-brenin Outdoor Pursuits Centre was opened. The National Eisteddfod of Wales was held at Pwllheli and the Cardiff-born poet R.S. Thomas won the prestigious Royal Literary Society's Heinemann Award. The main building of the National Library of Wales in Aberystwyth was completed and Anglesey became the first place in Britain to have fluoride added to its water supply.

In a game against Northern Ireland in Belfast, John and Mel Charles and Ivor and Len Allchurch became the first pair of brothers ever to play for Wales in the same team. Wales shared the rugby union championship with France while Barry Town won the Welsh Cup for the first time. In the second year of the award's existence, the athlete John Disley from Corris was voted Welsh Sports Personality of the Year. Dai Dower from Abercynon won the European flyweight title in London, and the Basketball Association of Wales was founded.

## BRITAIN AND IRELAND

Sir Winston Churchill resigned as Prime Minister and was replaced by Sir Anthony Eden while Clement Attlee handed over leadership of the Labour Party to Hugh Gaitskell. The Llanelli MP James Griffiths was elected deputy leader of the Labour Party. Independent Television was launched in London and the building of the first motorway was announced as well as the construction of the Ross Spur Road to improve links between the Midlands and South Wales. The government announced that Britain was to manufacture its own hydrogen bomb and Christopher Cockerell patented the prototype of his hovercraft.

In July, Ruth Ellis from Rhyl became the last woman to be hanged in Britain, and the death occurred of Sir Alexander Fleming, discoverer of penicillin. The year saw the births of Rowan Atkinson, Ian Botham, Elvis Costello, Steve Ovett and Sir Simon Rattle.

Equal pay for women teachers was introduced, blue jeans first went on sale in Britain and the Duke of Edinburgh Awards were instituted. There was a four week national dock strike in June which overlapped with a 17-day national rail strike and these had been preceded by a four week national newspaper strike from March to April. The basic travel allowance for trips abroad was retained at £100 a year, the first large group of Jamaicans arrived in Britain seeking work and in London Britain's first Wimpy bar was opened. The government annexed the tiny island of Rockall, 250 miles west of the Hebrides.

On Ullswater Donald Campbell set a new world water speed record of 202 mph and at Wembley Stadium the FA Cup was won by Newcastle United. The most popular British films of the year were *The Colditz Story*, *The Dambusters* and *The Ladykillers*. On television *This Is Your Life* was launched while Kingsley Amis's *That Uncertain Feeling* and Graham Greene's *The Quiet American* were published. *Rock Around the Clock* by Bill Haley and his Comets was a big record hit.

The Irish Republic became a member of the United Nations.

## THE WORLD

Ten years after the end of World War Two, Austria became a sovereign state again and West Germany joined NATO while in eastern Europe the Communist Warsaw Pact was established. The campaign for the union of Cyprus with Greece began with attacks on British troops based on the island.

At a meeting in Messina, Sicily, the Foreign Ministers of Belgium, France, Italy, Luxembourg, the Netherlands and West Germany agreed to integrate their economies, a decision that led to the present European Union of 25 members.

At the Le Mans motor racing circuit in France 80 spectators were killed and about 100 injured following a collision, while in Australia in March 200 people died in floods. In North Africa this was the first full year of the Algerian War of Independence and in West Germany the one millioneth Volkswagen Beetle rolled off the assembly lines.

In the USA the campaign against segregated bus seats began in Alabama while at Schenectady, New York, electricity was generated by atomic power for the first time anywhere in the world. In Argentina Juan Peron was overthrown and fled to Spain. The deaths occurred of Albert Einstein, of Thomas Mann the German novelist, of Charlie (Bird) Parker the jazz saxophonist, and of the young Hollywood film star James Dean who was killed in a car crash. The leading French painters Henri Matisse and Maurice Utrillo also died this year.

In Nepal the world's third highest mountain, Kanchenjunga (28,146 feet: 8,598 metres) was conquered by an expedition led by the Welshman Charles (later Sir Charles) Evans from Corwen. Disneyworld was opened in Los Angeles, the gymnast Olga Korbut was born in Russia, the film star Bruce Willis was born in Germany, Bill Gates founder of Microsoft was born in the USA, velcro was patented and the first Danish Lego sets went on sale. The Nobel Prize for Literature was won by the Icelandic writer Halldor Laxness and Sir Arthur Davies from Barry became head of the United Nations Meteorological Office in Geneva, a post he was to hold for 24 years.

Vladimir Nabukov's controversial novel *Lolita* was published and the Hollywood Oscar for Best Film went to *Marty* starring Ernest Borgnine. In New York a dramatisation of *The Diary of Ann Frank* was successfully staged.

# QUIZ SECTION

Many of the questions are based on information contained in earlier parts of this book.

## QUIZ ONE - CARDIFF IN 1905

*When Cardiff became a city this year* . . .

1.  was the New Theatre open ?
2.  had Cardiff's largest dock, the Alexandra, been opened ?
3.  had Ninian Park football ground been opened ?
4.  had Cardiff Rugby Club been formed ?
5.  was there still a horse-drawn bus service operating ?
6.  had Cardiff's first purpose-built cinema been opened ?
7.  was the Welsh Grand National being run at Ely Racecourse ?
8.  was Flat Holm being used as an isolation hospital ?
9.  had the Dowlais Works on East Moors begun producing steel ?
10. was James Howell's department store open ?
11. had a university college been established in Cardiff ?
12. was the Ferry Road tunnel under the River Ely to Penarth open ?
13. was there a Cardiff Royal Infirmary ?
14. had the Cardiff Coal and Shipping Exchange been opened?
15. had there been any airship flights from Cardiff ?
16. had any women been elected to the council ?
17. was the Animal Wall in place at the castle ?
18. was there any greyhound racing at the Arms Park ?
19. was there a Catholic Archbishop of Cardiff ?
20. was there a telephone service in Cardiff ?
21. had any of his four Olympic gold medals been won by the great Cardiff swimmer Paulo Radmilovich ?
22. had the first reservoir been constructed in the Brecon Beacons to supply water to Cardiff ?
23. was the *South Wales Echo* being published ?
24. had Roath Park been opened as a public park ?
25. were there any publicly-owned swimming baths in Cardiff ?
26. had the Hamadryad Hospital in the docks been opened ?
27. was Llandaff part of Cardiff ?
28. was the Pierhead Building in the docks open ?
29. had Maindy Barracks been opened ?

30. had the first Jewish synagogue in Cardiff been built ?
31. was Duke Street Arcade open ?
32. had house building on Cathedral Road been completed ?
33. was there a Cardiff City football club ?
34. were there any (Boy) Scouts and (Girl) Guides in Cardiff ?
35. had the South African War Memorial in Cathays Park been unveiled ?
36. had Cardiff hosted the first baseball international between England and Wales ?
37. was there a Gorsedd Circle in Cathays Park ?
38. was Cardiff the biggest place in Wales ?
39. were women still being hanged in Cardiff Prison ?
40. were pubs allowed to open on Sundays ?
41. was Cardiff's famous seal Billy living in Victoria Park lake ?
42. where was Temperance Town ?
43. where was Rat Island ?
44. where was the Cardiff Workhouse located ?
45. how many MPs represented Cardiff at Westminster ?
46. which one of these was not yet a public park
    (a) Hailey Park (b) Splott Park (c) Waterloo Gardens
    (d) Sophia Gardens ?
47. were there any municipal bowling greens ?
48. was there a zoo in Cardiff at this time ?
49. had Roath Harriers, the oldest athletic club in Wales, been formed ?
50. the population according to the 1901 census was approximately (a) 112,000 (b) 135,000 (c) 152,000 (d) 164,000 ?
51. what well-known Cardiff street was known as Plwcca Lane or Heol-y-plwcca until this year ?
52. had any of the buildings in the Civic Centre been erected ?
53. where was the statue of the second Marquis of Bute, now in Callaghan Square, then located ?
54. Galloway Races were regularly held at The Stadium in Grangetown. What were these races ?

55. was Glamorgan County Cricket Club playing county cricket games in the city ?

56. was any substantial part of the medieval town wall still standing ?

57. which one of these arcades was not yet open
(a) Castle Arcade (b) Dominions Arcade
(c) Wyndham Arcade (d) Morgan Arcade ?

58. had Llanishen Reservoir been built ?

59. had the Greek Orthodox Church in Bute Street been opened ?

60. had the construction of Castell Coch in Tongwynlais been completed ?

61. was there a museum in the town ?

62. were there any Labour Party members serving on the council ?

63. was the Mansion House in Richmond Road the official residence of the new Lord Mayor ?

64. was the Principality Building Society in existence ?

65. was the Glamorganshire Canal still in use ?

66. had the statue of John Bachelor in The Hayes been erected ?

67. had Brains Brewery been founded ?

68. Wood Street Congregational Church stood on the site of the present South Gate House and, as the largest place of worship in Wales, the number of people it could seat was (a) 2,000 (b) 3,000 (c) 4,000 (d) 5,000 ?

69. this was the last year for the operation of what sort of public transport service between Cardiff and Penarth
(a) a pony and trap service (b) a horse-drawn bus
(c) a steam ferryboat (d) a horse-drawn tram ?

70. which one of these statements about the National Eisteddfod of Wales and Cardiff is correct
(a) the Eisteddfod had been held there nine times
(b) the Eisteddfod had been held there six times
(c) the Eisteddfod had been held there twice
(d) the Eisteddfod had never been held there ?

*When Cardiff became the capital of Wales this year . . .*

1. were fishing trawlers still operating from the docks ?
2. was the Prince of Wales (now a pub) still in use as a theatre ?
3. had Jacob Epstein's statue *Christ in Majesty* in Llandaff Cathedral been consecrated ?
4. was there a local commercial television service ?
5. were pubs allowed to open on Sundays ?
6. had the first searchlight tattoo been held in the castle ?
7. was coal still being shipped out of the docks ?
8. were city centre shops still closing for a half day on Wednesday ?
9. were there any traffic wardens on duty in the city ?
10. were trolley buses still running ?
11. was there a hospital at The Heath ?
12. where was Glamorgan playing its county cricket games - Sophia Gardens or the Arms Park?
13. were pleasure steamers sailing from Pierhead ?
14. was Cardiff Airport still at Pengam ?
15. did Ninian Park have floodlights ?
16. were cinemas allowed to open on Sundays ?
17. had Thornhill Crematorium been opened ?
18. were there any betting shops in the city ?
19. was the school leaving age (a) 13 (b) 14 (c) 15 (d) 16 ?
20. was any part of the Glamorganshire Canal in the city still in use ?
21. did Cardiff Castle still belong to the Bute family ?
22. was there still greyhound racing at the Arms Park ?
23. were executions still being carried out in Cardiff Prison ?
24. were young men still being called up for compulsory military service ?
25. was the annual South Wales Miners' Gala being held in the city ?
26. was the Taff Swim race still being held ?
27. was the Museum of Welsh Life (the Folk Museum) open at St Fagans ?

28. were Whitchurch, Rhiwbina and Radyr part of the city ?
29. had the BBC studios and offices been opened at Llandaff ?
30. was the Norwegian Church still a consecrated building used for religious services ?
31. was there still a pedestrian subway open under the River Ely linking Ferry Road with Penarth ?
32. was the Central Bus Station open ?
33. was Cardiff City playing in the (then) First Division of the Football League ?
34. was the Cardiff Coal and Shipping Exchange still functioning as a business centre ?
35. had the city ever had a woman Lord Mayor ?
36. had the Welsh Industrial and Maritime Musem been opened in the docks area ?
37. was there a Welsh College of Music and Drama in the city ?
38. had any Welsh medium primary schools been opened in the city ?
39. was there an HMS *Cardiff* in the Royal Navy ?
40. was there an HMS *Llandaff* in the Royal Navy ?
41. had Welsh National Opera been founded in the city ?
42. was it possible to play ten pin bowling anywhere in the city ?
43. had Capital Tower on the corner of Greyfriars Road and The Friary been constructed ?
44. had the Urdd Gobaith Cymru National Eisteddfod ever been held in the city ?
45. what was in the building which is now the Cardiff Hilton Hotel ?
46. had the flats on the western side of Westgate Street been constructed ?
47. how many MPs represented the city at Westminster ?
48. was Manor Way road open ?
49. was there still a Merchant Navy Hotel in the city ?

50. what was the name of the Royal Navy Volunteer Reserve minesweeper based in the docks (a) HMS *Red Dragon* (b) HMS *St David* (c) HMS *Daffodil* (d) HMS *Merlin* ?

51. the city's population according to the 1951 census was (a) 246,000 (b) 205,000 (c) 171,000 (d) 164,000 ?

52. what was the name of the present Cardiff Central Station then ?

53. was the city's largest sports and recreational area, Trelai Park, open ?

54. was there a Gorsedd Circle in Bute Park ?

55. which one of these Cardiff statues had not yet been erected (a) Aneurin Bevan (Queen Street) (b) Lord Aberdare (Alexandra Gardens) (c) the third Marquis of Bute (Friary Gardens) (d) Lord Tredegar (Boulevard de Nantes) ?

56. had Western Avenue been opened ?

57. was the *Cardiff Queen* paddle steamer operating in the Bristol Channel ?

58. was Sophia Gardens Pavilion in use for concerts, dances and exhibitions ?

59. was there a 50 metre swimming pool in the city ?

60. the number of cinemas (all single screen) open in the city was (a) 27 (b) 21 (c) 15 (d) 11 ?

61. was corporal punishment still being used in the city's schools ?

62. was speedway racing taking place in the city ?

63. was there a manned lighthouse on Flat Holm ?

64. was there still a farm on Flat Holm ?

65. had Chapter Arts Centre in Canton been opened ?

66. were the Dowlais Works on East Moors still producing steel ?

67. were Lord Mayor's Parades being held in the city ?

68. were major agricultural shows still being held in the city ?

69. was Llandaff Technical College on Western Avenue open ?

70. was the 11 plus examination being used to select children for secondary education ?

## QUIZ THREE - CARDIFF NOW

*In contemporary Cardiff . . .*

1. which one of these well-known Welsh actors was not born in the city - (a) Ioan Gruffudd (b) Angharad Rees (c) Rhys Ifans (d) Matthew Rhys ?

2. which is the tallest of these structures (a) the Castle Clock Tower (b) St John's Church Tower (c) the City Hall Clock Tower (d) the Wales Millennium Centre ?

3. which is the older - the St David's Shopping Centre or the Capitol Shopping Centre ?

4. which has the largest seating capacity (a) The New Theatre (b) St David's Hall (c) Wales Millennium Centre (d) Cardiff International Arena ?

5. name the two internationally famous female singing stars born in Cardiff - one in 1937 and the other in 1986.

6. which one of these well-known footballers was not born in the city - (a) Ryan Giggs (b) Mark Hughes (c) John Toshack (d) Terry Yorath ?

7. which one of these Cardiff-born sports personalities has not won an Olympic medal (a) Tanni Grey-Thompson (b) Colin Jackson (c) Nigel Walker (d) Martin Woodroffe (e) David Broome ?

8. which one of these leading rugby personalities was not born in the city - (a) Gareth Edwards (b) Terry Holmes (c) Gareth Llywellyn (d) J.P.R.Williams ?

9. which one of these best-selling novelists was not born in the city - (a) Ken Follett (b) Dick Francis (c) Bernice Rubens (d) Craig Thomas ?

10. which one of these well-known broadcasting personalities was born in the city - (a) Martyn Lewis (b) John Humphrys (c) Huw Edwards (d) Roy Noble ?

11. which one of these Glamorgan and England cricketers was born in the city - (a) Robert Croft (b) Matthew Maynard (c) Tony Lewis (d) Hugh Morris ?

70

12. which one of these Welsh show business personalities was not born in the city (a) Tom Jones (b) Griff Rhys Jones (c) Stan Stennett (d) Shakin' Stevens ?

13. name the multi-cultural annual festival which began in the docks area in 1990.

14. the length of the Bute Tunnel (A4232) in Cardiff Bay is (a) 550 metres (600 yards) (b) 610 metres (670 yards) (c) 715 metres (780 yards) (d) 825 metres(960 yards) ?

15. which leading Welsh politician opened the Taff Viaduct and the Bute Tunnel in 1995 (a) Peter Hain (b) Neil Kinnock (c) Rhodri Morgan (d) Jim Callaghan ?

16. what low cost airline began operating from Cardiff International Airport in 2002 (a) EasyJet (b) bmibaby (c) Go (d) Ryanair ?

17. which one of these is not in the city (a) St David's Cathedral (b) St David's Hall (c) St David's College (d) St David's Hospital ?

18. where is the Cardiff World Trade Centre to be found ?

19. which one of these Welsh national figures is not represented in the City Hall's Marble Hall of eleven statues (a) Saint David (b) David Lloyd George (c) Owain Glyndŵr (d) William Williams, Pantycelyn ?

20. which one of these Cardiff roads was opened in 1971 (a) the Docks Link Road (b) the Gabalfa flyover (c) the Grangetown Link Road (d) the Ely Link Road ?

21. in which year was the biennial BBC Singer of the World Cardiff competition launched (a) 1983 (b) 1987 (c) 1991 (d) 1993 ?

22. which one of these Cardiff hotels has the most rooms and which the fewest (a) The Hilton (b) Jury's (c) The Marriott d) The Angel ?

23. which one of these bus companies runs the open top bus tours of the city (a) National Express (b) Shamrock (c) Stagecoach (d) City Sightseeing ?

24. the number of screens in the UGC Cinema in Mary Ann Street is (a) 10 (b) 12 (c) 15 (d) 18 ?

25. the length of the Taff Trail for walkers and cyclists between Cardiff and Brecon is (a) 40 miles (64 kilometres) (b) 55 miles (88 kilometres)(c) 65 miles (105 kilometres) (d) 80 miles (128 kilometres) ?

26. what major Welsh festival is taking place in the city in 2008 ?

27. what is the name of the annual musical festival which began in the city in 2002 ?

28. where in the city is there a Celtic Cross memorial dedicated in 1999 to the victims of the Irish potato famine of the 1840s ?

29. what were the original names given to Lloyd George Avenue and Callaghan Square ?

30. where in the city is the Celtic Ring ?

31. which one of these animals is not depicted on the Animal Wall at the Castle (a) bear (b) stag (c) sea lion (d) lynx ?

32. the offices of the British Boxing Board of Control are located in which building in the centre of the city ?

33. what organisation now has its offices in Plas Glyndŵr on Kingsway which was formerly the Bank of Wales building ?

34. where in the city in one place will you find these Cardiff-born sports personalities honoured: Jim Sullivan (rugby league), Jack Petersen (boxing), Billy Boston (rugby league) and Jim Driscoll (boxing) ?

35. according to the 2001 census the city's population was approximately (a) 275,000 (b) 295,000 (c) 305,000 (d) 325,000 ?

36. the biennial Cardiff Artes Mundi prize for visual arts, first awarded in 2004, is worth how much to the winner (a) £10,000 (b) £20,000 (c) £30,000 (d) £40,000 ?

37. where in the city are the headquarters of the Welsh youth movement Urdd Gobaith Cymru ?

32. where are the studios of Real Radio ?

39. where are the studios of Red Dragon Radio ?

40. which of the city's hotels was once considered to be a ship ?

41. what is the area of the Cardiff Bay lake (a) 1,000 acres (400 hectares) (b) 500 acres (200 hectares) (c) 250 acres (100 hectares) (d) 100 acres (50 hectares) ?

42. where was the Norwegian Church located before it was removed to its present position in Cardiff Bay ?

43. which one of these city parks does not have a lake (a) Roath Park (b) Victoria Park (c) Wern Goch Park (d) Bute Park ?

44. what is the name of the former lightship permanently moored in Roath Basin and which is now a Christian centre ?

45. where is The Donald Gordon Theatre ?

46. where in the city will you find a memorial to Raoul Wallenberg, the Swedish diplomat who saved many thousands of Hungarian Jews from Nazi concentration camps at the end of World War Two ?

47. according to the 2001 census, the population of the city which is Welsh-speaking is (a) 2 per cent (b) 5 per cent (c) 12 per cent (d) 22 per cent ?

48. which one .of these new city apartment blocks is not on the Cardiff Bay lakeside (a) Ocean Reach (b) Prospect Place (c) Sovereign Quay (d) Altolusso ?

49 which one of these city buildings has not received money from the National Lottery (a) Cardiff Castle (b) Wales Millennium Stadium (c) Wales Millennium Centre (d) The Hilton Hotel ?

50. what is the seating capacity of the new 50 metre swimminq pool at the Cardiff International Sports Village (a) 2,100 (b) 1,400 (c) 900 (d) 500 ?

51. where in the city are the statues of the leading Welsh sports personalities Jim Driscoll and Gareth Edwards?

52. what Scandinavian company opened a major store in the city in 2003 ?

53. by how many MPs is Cardiff represented in Westminster ?

54. how many Welsh medium comprehensive high schools are there in the city ?

55. what was the building which is now The Aspect apartment block at the eastern end of Queen Street originally built as ?

55. what new hospital was opened in the city in 2002 ?

57. which was the last of these cinemas to open in the city (a) UGC (b) Ster Century (c) UCI (d) Chapter ?

58. name the new Welsh airline which began operating from Cardiff International Airport in 2001.

59. what first appeared on the lawn outside the City Hall during the 2001-2002 winter ?

60. what is the name of the new city centre development between St Mary Street and Caroline Street ?

61. how many comprehensive high schools are in the city (a) 32 (b) 26 (c) 20 (d) 14 ?

62. what European title did the city fail to win in 2003 in competition with Birmingham, Bristol, Liverpool (the winners), Newcastle-Gateshead and Oxford?

63. where are the studios of S4C, the Welsh language television channel ?

64. what is the approximate seating capacity of the Wales National Ice Rink (a) 900 (b) 1,800 (c) 2,500 (d) 4,200 ?

65. what was Roald Dahls Plass in Cardiff Bay known as before this name was officially introduced in 2002 ?

66. the former Allied Steel and Wire (ASW) works were closed in 2002 and the plant was reopened by Celsa in 2003. Is this new company (a) Italian (b) Spanish (c) Dutch (e) French ?

67. which one of these city hotels is not four star (a) The Copthorne, Culverhouse Cross (b) The Hanover International, Schooner Way (c) The Holiday Inn, Castle Street (e) The Marriott, Mill Lane ?

68. which one of these regimental museums is in Cardiff Castle (a) The Welsh Guards (b) The Royal Welch Fusiliers (c) The South Wales Borderers (d) The Welch Regiment ?

69. which one of these statements about the Cardiff Bay barrage is incorrect - (a) it is 1,200 yards (1,100 metres) long (b) it took over 5 years to construct it (c) it is not as long as the Thames Barrier (d) it has impounded the waters of the River Taff and the River Ely ?

70. the approximate area of the city is (a) 28 square miles (11,000 hectares) (b) 36 square miles (14,000 hectares) (c) 73 square miles (19,000 hectares) (d) 86 square miles (33,000 hectares) ?

# QUIZ ONE - CARDIFF IN 1905 - ANSWERS

1. No - not until 1906.
2. No - it was opened in 1907.
3. No - it was opened in 1910.
4. Yes - it was formed in 1876.
5. No - it ended in 1902 with the introduction of electric trams.
6. No - the 'Electra' was opened in Queen Street in 1909.
7. Yes - from 1895 to 1939. (It is now run at Chepstow).
8. Yes - from 1896 to 1935.
9. Yes - from 1891.
10. Yes - Howell's opened in 1865.
11 Yes - it was founded in 1883.
12- Yes - it was opened in 1900.
13. No - not until 1923, before that it was the Cardiff Infirmary.
14. Yes - it opened in 1886.
15. Yes - just seven weeks before Cardiff became a city E.T.Willows made his first flight.
16. No - the first woman was not elected to the council until 1920.
17. Yes - but not where it is now: it was moved from in front of the castle in 1926.
18. No - not until 1928.
19. No - not until 1916.
20. Yes - from 1877.
21. No -'Raddy' won Olympic golds in 1908, 1912 and 1920.
22. Yes - it was finished in 1892.
23. Yes - it was launched in 1886.
24. Yes - it was opened in 1894.
25. Yes - Guildford Crescent Baths (now the site of the Ibis Hotel) opened in 1896.
26. No - it was not opened until 1906, replacing the ship *Hamadryad*, which had served as a seamen's hospital since 1860.
27. No - not until 1922.
28. Yes - it was opened in 1897 by the Bute family.
29. Yes - the barracks were opened in 1881.
30. Yes - it was opened in 1858 near Charles Street.
31. Yes - it was opened in 1902.
32. Yes - the houses were built between 1880 and 1900.
33. No - Riverside Football Club was founded in 1899 but was not renamed Cardiff City until 1908.
34. No - the first Scout troop was founded in 1908 and the first Guides in 1914.
35. No - not until 1909 when it was unveiled by General Sir John French.
36. No - the first international was not played until 1908.
37. Yes - it was erected for the 1899 National Eisteddfod of Wales.
38. Yes - and had been since 1871 when, with a population of 57,363, it overtook Merthyr Tydfil
39. Yes - the last execution of a woman in Cardiff Prison took place in 1907.
40. No - the Sunday closing of pubs in Wales had been introduced in 1881.
41. No - Billy (actually a female) lived in Victoria Park Lake from 1912 to her death in 1939. (A statue of Billy was unveiled in the park in 1997).
42. The area around the present Central Bus Station.
43. The area in the docks between the Glamorganshire Canal and the River Taff.
44. It was on the site of the new St David's Hospital on Cowbridge Road.
45. One MP only.
46. (a) Hailey Park - it was not opened until 1926.
47. Yes - the first was opened in Victoria Park in 1905.
48. Yes - there was a zoo or menagerie in Victoria Park from 1900 to 1941.
49. Yes - the Harriers were formed in 1882.

50. (d) 164,000
51. City Road.
52. Yes - the University Registry (1903) and the City Hall and the Law Courts (both in 1904).
53. It was at the bottom of St Mary Street where the short length of dual carriageway now begins.
54. Races for small horses less than 15 hands high.
55. Yes - but Minor Counties cricket only: Glamorgan was not admitted to the County Cricket Championship until 1921.
56. No - the last part, in Kingsway, was demolished in 1901.
57. (b) Dominions Arcade - it did not open until 1921.
58. Yes - it was built in the 1880s.
59. No - it was not opened until 1906.
60. Yes - it was completed in 1887.
61. Yes - the museum was in the.Central Library (the Old Library) opened in 1882.

62. No - the first four were not elected until 1919.
63. No - not until 1913. (It had been the residence of the department store owner James Howell. It ceased being the Lord Mayor's official residence in 1999).
64. Yes - it was founded in 1860.
65. Yes - the canal was still in use but only the length between Cardiff and Abercynon. (The Abercynon-Merthyr Tydfil part of the canal was closed in 1898 and the Aberdare branch was closed in 1900).
66. Yes - it was unveiled in 1866.
67. Yes - the brewery was founded in 1882.
68 (b) 3,000 (it was demolished in 1972)
69 (c) a steam ferryboat.
70 (c) the Eisteddfod had been held there twice - in 1883 and in 1899.

**77**

## QUIZ TWO - CARDIFF IN 1955 - ANSWERS

1. Yes - the last fishing vessels were laid up in 1956.
2. Yes - until 1956 when it became a cinema.
3. No - it was consecrated in 1957.
4. No - not until 1958 when TWW (Television Wales and the West) was launched.
5. No - not until 1961.
6. No - the first tattoo was in 1963 and the last in 1987.
7. Yes - until 1964.
8. Yes - until 1965.
9. No - there were no traffic wardens until 1964.
10. Yes - they did not finish running until 1970.
11. No - the Dental Hospital was opened in 1966 and the General Hospital in 1971.
12. At the Arms Park until 1967 and since 1968 at Sophia Gardens.
13. Yes - the service ended in 1972.
14. No - the move to Rhoose took place in 1954.
15. No - not until 1960.
16. Yes - since 1952.
17. Yes - it opened in 1953.
18. No - there were no betting shops until 1961.
19. (c) 15 - it was raised to this age from 14 in 1947 and raised to 16 in 1973.
20. No - the last part, the sea lock, closed in 1951 after a collision with a dredger and the last barge travelled on it in 1943.
21. No - the Butes gave it to Cardiff in 1947.
22. Yes - greyhound racing did not end until 1977.
23. No - the last execution was in 1952.
24- Yes - young men were being conscripted until the end of 1960.
25. Yes - they began in 1954.
26. Yes - until 1961 but in Roath Park Lake not the River Taff from where the event had been moved in 1931.
27. Yes - it opened in 1948.
28. No - not until 1967.
29. No - they were still in Park Place until 1967.
30. Yes - the last service was held there in 1974.
31. Yes - the tunnel was not closed until 1963. (It had been opened in 1900).
32. Yes - it opened in 1954.
33. Yes - Cardiff City was promoted from the (then) Second Division in 1952.
34. Yes - the Exchange was not closed until 1958.
35. No - the first woman Lord Mayor, Mrs Helena Evans, took office in 1959.
36. No - the Museum was not opened until 1977.(It was demolished in 1992 to make way for the Mermaid Quay development in the Bay).
37. Yes - it was in Cardiff Castle from where it was moved to North Road in 1975.
38. Yes - the first opened at Ninian Park in 1949 with 18 pupils.
39. No - the light cruiser HMS *Cardiff* was broken up in 1946 and the guided missile destroyer HMS *Cardiff* was not launched until 1979.
40. Yes - the frigate HMS *Llandaff* was launched in 1955. (She was decommissioned in 1976).
41. Yes - in 1946.
42. No - not until 1988 in Newport Road.
43. No - Capital Tower was not opened until 1970. (It was originally known as the Pearl Building).
44. No - it was first held in Cardiff in 1965.

45. It was the Prudential Building, an office block opened in 1952.
46. Yes - the flats were built in the 1930s.
47. Three MPs.
48. No - it was built between 1957 and 1959.
49. Yes - it was later renamed the Station Hotel and demolished in 1994.
50. HMS *St David*.(She was based in the city until 1961).
51. (a) 246,000.
52. Cardiff General Station.
53. Yes - it opened in 1953.
54. No - it was erected in 1977 for the 1978 National Eisteddfod.
55. (a) Aneurin Bevan - it was unveiled in 1987.
56. Yes - it was opened in 1933.
57. Yes - she was launched on the Clyde in 1947 and not taken out of service until 1966.
58. Yes - from 1951. (A converted RAF hanger, it was demolished in 1982).
59. No - not until the Wales Empire Pool was opened in 1958. (It was demolished in 1998).

60. (b) 21.
61. Yes, it was not abolished until 1984.
62. No - speedway racing ended at Penarth Road in 1953.
63. Yes - it was manned until 1988 when it became automatic.
64. No - farming was abandoned in 1941 during World War Two when a 350-strong military garrison was based on the island.
65. No - Chapter was not opened until 1972.
66. Yes - steel making did not end there until 1978.
67. No - the first parade was in 1961 and the last in 2001.
68. Yes - the Bath and West Show was held in Cardiff in 1958, its thirteenth and last visit.(The last Royal Welsh Show was in 1953).
69. Yes - it opened in 1954 but the site is now the Llandaff Campus of UWIC - University of Wales Institute Cardiff.
70. Yes - it was not abolished until 1964.

1. (c) Rhys Ifans who was born in Pembrokeshire.
2. (c) City Hall Clock Tower, 197 feet (60 metres).
3. St David's Shopping Centre, 1982. (Capitol Shopping Centre 1990).
4. Cardiff International Arena with a 5,500 seating capacity.
5. Dame Shirley Bassey was born in 1937 and Charlotte Church in 1986.
6. (b) Mark Hughes who was born in Rhosllanerchrugog.
7. (c) Nigel Walker.
8. (a) Gareth Edwards who was born in Gwaun-cae-gurwen.
9. (b) Dick Francis who was born in Tenby.
10. (b) John Humphrys.
11. (d) Hugh Morris.
12. (a) Tom Jones who was born in Treforest.
13. MAS Carnival.
14. (c) 715 metres (780 yards).
15. (b) Neil Kinnock.
16. (b) bmibaby.
17. (c) St David's College - it is in Lampeter.
18. In the Cardiff International Arena (CIA) in Mary Ann Street.
19. (b) David Lloyd George who unveiled all the statues in 1916.
20. (b) the Gabalfa flyover in 1971.
21. (a) 1983.
22. The Hilton Hotel the most with 197 rooms and the Angel the fewest with 102 rooms.
23. (d) City Sightseeing.
24. (c) 15.
25. (b) 55 miles (88 kilometres).
26. The Royal National Eisteddfod of Wales.
27. The Cardiff Worldport Festival.
28. In Cathays Cemetery.
29. Bute Avenue and Bute Square.
30. It is at the mouth of Roald Dahls Plass marking the start of the Taff Trail between Cardiff and Brecon.
31. (b) stag.
32. In the Old Library.
33. The Welsh Development Agency. (To be abolished by 2006)
34. At the Welsh Sports Hall of Fame, Museum of Welsh Life, St Fagans.
35. (c) 305,000.
36. (d) £40,000 - it is one of the richest art prizes in the world.
37. In the Wales Millennium Centre. (Formerly in Conway Road, Canton).
38. In Morganstown.
39. In the Atlantic Wharf Leisure Village.
40. The United States Navy took over the Angel Hotel in 1917 and renamed it USS *Chattinouka*.
41. (b) 500 acres (200 hectares).
42. At the southern end of the former Bute West Dock on the site of the Atlantic Wharf Leisure Village.
43. (d) Bute Park does not have a lake.
44. The *Helwick*.
45. In the Wales Millenniun Centre: the 1,900 seat theatre is named after the South African millionaire who gave £10 million to the project.
46. In Alexandra Gardens, Cathays Park - it was unveiled in 1985.
47. (c) 12 per cent.
48. (d) Altolusso is in Bute Terrace.
49. (d) The Hilton Hotel.
50. (c) 900.
51. Jim Driscoll's statue is in Bute Terrace and that of Gareth Edwards is in the St David's Centre.
52. IKEA. (It was the company's 12th and second largest store in Britain).

53. Four MPs.
54. Two - at Llandaff North and at Plasmawr.
55. It was the Automobile Association (AA) office block.
56. St David's Hospital, Cowbridge Road.
57. (b) Ster Century in 2003.
58. Air Wales.
59. An open-air ice skating rink.
60. The Brewery Quarter.
61. (c) 20 comprehensive high schools.
62. European City of Culture but Cardiff was designated a UK Centre of Culture.
63. Parc Ty Glas, Llanishen.
64. (c) 2,500.
65. The Oval Basin.
66. (b) Spanish - based in Barcelona.
67. (c) The Holiday Inn, Castle Street is three star.
68. (d) The Welch Regiment Museum - it was opened in 1978.
69. (c) is incorrect: at 520 metres the Thames Barrier is half the length of the barrage.
70. (b) 36 square miles (14,000 hectares). (a) is the area of Merthyr Tydfil, (c) is the area of Newport and (d) is the area of the Vale of Glamorgan.

# SUGGESTIONS FOR FURTHER READING

## Non-Fiction

Chappell, Edgar L.    *The History of the Port of Cardiff*
                      (second edition)                        (1994)
Davies, John          *A Pocket Guide to Cardiff*              (2002)
Dicks, Brian          *Cardiff and its Valleys*               (1984)
Finch, Peter          *Real Cardiff*                          (2002)
Gillham, Mary E.      *A Natural History of Cardiff*          (2002)
Hillings, J.B.        *Cardiff and the Valleys*               (1973)
Jenkins, J. Geraint and Jenkins, David
                      *Cardiff Shipowners*                    (1986)
Morgan, Dennis        *The Cardiff Story* (second edition) (2004)
Morgan, Dennis        *Discovering Cardiff's Past*            (1995)
Morgan, Rhodri        *Cardiff: Half-and-Half a Capital*      (1994)
Stephens, Meic (editor) *A Cardiff Anthology*                 (1987)

## Fiction

Azzopardi, Trezza     *The Hiding Place*                      (2000)
Jones, Jack           *River Out of Eden*                     (1951)
Williams, John        *Five Pubs, Two Bars and a Nightclub*
                                                              (1999)
Williams, John        *Cardiff Dead*                          (2001)
Williams, John        *The Prince of Wales*                   (2003)

# CARDIFF
# GUIDED TOURS

Take a closer look at Cardiff
by booking a guided walking tour
of the city centre.

Individuals and groups welcome for
a two mile walk taking in
the Civic Centre,
the Castle grounds,
the Millennium Stadium's Riverside Walk
and the medieval town centre.

The tour is wheelchair accessible.

For bookings and inquiries
telephone 029 2081 1603, or
fax 029 2081 1049

**The Professional Service
for Visitors**